Richard Harris & Christoper

Build Up Reading | Level 2

Richard Harris & Christoper

Cover/Interior Design: Design YoungZoo

ISBN: 978-89-90545-68-8

Desk Copy Request / Information
To place your desk copy request or for more information,
please contact the following office:
Tel: (02)3273-4300   Fax: (02)3273-4303
Homepage : www.wcbooks.co.kr

Contents

01 THE CHANGING WORLD

1. What is continental drift?
2. What happens when a volcano erupts on the floor of the ocean?
3. Why is the Pacific Ocean becoming bigger?

 T1

1 No one knows exactly what the origin of the Earth is. But many leading scientists agree that the Earth was all one gigantic landmass about 300 million years ago. All the **continents** were connected together and were called Gondwana. Approximately 200 million years ago, this landmass began breaking up. The continents then began **drifting** apart, at a snail's pace, eventually ending up in their present position. This theory is now referred to as continental drift. Between all the continents were **massive** holes and canyons that filled up with water over time. One of these "trenches," the one between the Americas and Africa eventually widened and became known as the Atlantic Ocean.

2 But the continents and ocean floor are gradually changing. In the middle of the Earth lies a center made of liquid rock that is very hot. It's so hot that continents move because of the **intense** heat underneath them. They actually float on this liquid rock. Once in a while, when the hot molten material breaks through to the surface, a volcano **erupts**. When volcanoes erupt on the bottom of the ocean, the water cools the molten lava into rock. This leads to the lava cooling and becoming part of the Earth's crust, at which time the rock is pushed farther and farther apart.

3 In other words, the Earth's crust is just like a giant pie, constantly changing with small eruptions on its surface. Because many volcanoes continuously erupt at the bottom of the Pacific Ocean these days, more and more new crusts are forming. The result is that the continents are slowly being pushed together. The Pacific Ocean is getting bigger, while the Atlantic Ocean is getting smaller.

4 Today the continents are drifting toward one another contrary to what happened 200 million years ago. However, this process is so slow that hardly anyone notices it is happening. And yet in another 200 million years, it just might be possible to drive from the United States to Africa in a car!

Vocabulary Study

A **Choose and write the correct word.**

> drifting   massive   intense   erupt   continents

1. The water was boiling for a long time, so the heat was very ___________.

2. Asia is a truly ___________ continent.

3. I have never seen a volcano ___________ before.

4. The ship was ___________ on the sea because it couldn't use its motor.

5. People in America believe there are seven ___________ in the world.

B **Replace the underlined words with a synonym from the box.**

> gigantic   forms   approximately   possible   eventually

1. The continents <u>ultimately</u> stopped drifting.

2. It is not <u>plausible</u> to drive from New York to Cairo.

3. Atlantis was a <u>huge</u> island.

4. <u>Roughly</u> 500 people attended the conference.

5. Our vision <u>shapes</u> our future.

Main idea

This story is about ______________.

   a. oceans   b. continental drift

   c. volcanoes   d. Earth

Paragraph Understanding

Choose the correct answer.

1. Paragraph ___   When lava cools underwater, it becomes part of the Earth's crust.
2. Paragraph ___   The Atlantic Ocean is actually shrinking.
3. Paragraph ___   Today the continents are moving toward each other.
4. Paragraph ___   Scientists have a theory called continental drift.

Looking for detail

Circle the correct answer.

1. Long ago, at what speed did the continents drift apart?
   a. Very slowly
   b. Somewhat slowly
   c. Somewhat fast
   d. Very fast

2. New crusts are continually forming in oceans because of ___________.
   a. water
   b. weather patterns
   c. volcanoes
   d. the continents

3. Which paragraph talks about what happens at the middle of the Earth?
   a. Paragraph 1
   b. Paragraph 2
   c. Paragraph 3
   d. Paragraph 4

4. When lava cools and becomes part of the Earth's crust, ___________.
   a. it explodes above the surface
   b. it breaks through the surface to the continents
   c. it pushes the water down to the middle of the Earth
   d. it pushes the rock around it farther and farther apart

Developing Skills

Find a grammatical mistake and correct it.

1. About 300 million years ago, the Earth is one huge landmass.

   ____

2. The middle of the Earth is call the core.

   ____

3. Despite the Pacific Ocean is getting bigger, the Atlantic Ocean is getting smaller.

   ____

4. These days the continents are drift toward each other.

   ____

5. Some day I drove from Miami to Egypt!

   ____

 T2 **Summary & Listening Practice**

**Read the paragraph and fill in as many blanks as you can.
Then listen to the recording and fill in the rest of the blanks.**

A very long time ago, the continents started drifting ① ____________ from each other. Soon, water ② ____________ the huge spaces between the continents. In the Pacific Ocean today, volcanoes often ③ ____________. When the water cools, the molten ④ ____________ is turned into rock. This adds to the Earth's crust, pushing the rock farther and farther apart. As a result, the Americas and Africa are gradually being ⑤ ____________ together.

 T3

1. One of the most amazing victories in ancient Greek times involved a small group of men, a clever idea, and a huge wooden horse. Today we know this story as the Trojan War because of an ancient Greek poem by the renowned writer Homer. The story tells the tale of a Trojan prince falling in love with Helen, the wife of a Greek king. He took her back to his home in Troy, a decision that greatly angered the Greeks. Eventually, the Greeks **declared** war against Troy.

2. After 10 years, however, the war was still not won. The city of Troy was so well protected that the Greeks had not been able to penetrate the outer city walls. Then the Greeks came up with a very creative idea. They **pretended** to give up, leaving a huge wooden horse as a gift for the people of Troy. Later, after the Greeks were thought to have sailed away, the horse was taken into the walled city of Troy. At night, Greek soldiers who had been hiding inside the horse came out and opened the main gates. They let in the rest of their army and captured Troy. Their trick had worked!

3. No one knows whether this tale is true or not because for a long time, the **remains** of a wooden horse were never found. But in the 19th century, archaeologists found the remains of Troy. They discovered many layers in the ruins, concluding that Troy had risen and fallen many times over thousands of years. Still, the question left unanswered is: What had made Troy such an important place?

4. Troy's **location** is most likely the answer. It was built on a strait between the Mediterranean Sea and the Black Sea, in an area called the Dardanelles (now modern day Turkey). Because the current is very strong there, ships would have to wait until the wind was behind them to proceed further. This could sometimes take weeks and was expensive for the sailors as they had to pay a heavy **toll** to moor their ships. If the Greeks got tired of paying a fee to wait, they would probably just fight against the Trojans instead. Thus, the battle over Troy was likely due to money, not a woman.

Vocabulary Study

A Choose and write the correct word.

location toll remains declared pretended

1. We had to pay an expensive ___________ on the highway.

2. Before leaving the airport, Robert ___________ his duty-free goods.

3. The ___________ of the dead woman were buried in the cemetery.

4. All the children ___________ to be monsters for Halloween.

5. The pizza store moved its ___________ closer to my house.

B Replace the underlined words with a synonym from the box.

famous penetrated discovered give up founded

1. Several men <u>entered</u> the village.

2. Troy was <u>built</u> in an area called Dardanelles.

3. The remains of the Trojan horse were not <u>found</u>.

4. Homer was a very <u>well-known</u> Greek poet.

5. The Greeks pretended to <u>surrender</u>.

Main idea

This story is about ___________.

   a. a poet   b. a war

   c. an army   d. new languages and cultures

02

Paragraph Understanding

Choose the correct answer.

1. Paragraph ___   The Greeks played a trick and it worked.
2. Paragraph ___   We know about the Trojan War because of a poem.
3. Paragraph ___   The remains of Troy were discovered in the 1800s.
4. Paragraph ___   People had to pay a heavy toll while waiting at Troy.

Looking for detail

Circle the correct answer.

1. Who was Helen originally married to?
   - a. A Greek king
   - b. A Greek prince
   - c. A Trojan king
   - d. A Trojan prince

2. Greek soldiers hid inside a wooden horse and came out ___________.
   - a. in the morning
   - b. in the early evening
   - c. in the afternoon
   - d. at night

3. Which paragraph talks about where Troy is?
   - a. Paragraph 1
   - b. Paragraph 2
   - c. Paragraph 3
   - d. Paragraph 4

4. What might be discovered in the future?
   - a. Helen's remains
   - b. Homer's remains
   - c. The remains of a Trojan prince
   - d. The remains of the Trojan Horse

Developing Skills

Find a grammatical mistake and correct it.

1. Greek soldiers fought during ten years before pretending to leave.

   ____

2. Troy is locates between the Mediterranean Sea and the Black Sea.

   ____

3. The Greeks played a very successful tricks on the Trojans.

   ____

4. I'd like reading the poem about the Trojan War.

   ____

5. I hope that archeologists finding the remains of the Trojan Horse some day.

   ____

T4   Summary & Listening Practice

Read the paragraph and fill in as many blanks as you can.
Then listen to the recording and fill in the rest of the blanks.

According to a Greek poem, a long time ago a Trojan prince fell in love with a Greek queen, and took her back to his home in Troy. For 10 years, the Greeks ① ____________ tried to get inside the city walls. Only when they ② ____________ to leave, giving the Trojans a wooden horse as a ③ ____________, did the Greeks finally get inside Troy. Today, archeologists and historians aren't sure if a wooden horse ever existed. However, they have found the ④ ____________ of Troy, so they know it was once a real city that was ⑤ ____________ in the Dardanelles.

03   The Importance of Playing with Animals

 T5

1. Nothing is cuter than a young puppy or kitten. But did you know that during these early months and years, these cuddly animals are doing much more than playing? Well, as it turns out, these young animals are actually learning when they play? Just like going to a type of "school." While they play, the brains send messages to the muscles. This **strengthens** their balance and muscle control. By playing when they are young, animals practice and develop behavior they will need later on as adults.

2. Although not as important in **domestic** pets that we keep at home, behavior learned while playing as a youngster can be the difference between survival and death. You may have seen this before, but lambs or baby deer might suddenly start to run across a meadow or through a forest for no **obvious** reason. They are reacting to sounds in their environment. This helps develop behavior that they might one day need when escaping from a predator like a wolf or mountain lion.

3. Even the young of much larger and stronger animals like lions and wolves need practice, too. If their baby animals don't learn how to hunt when they are young, they may not be able to **feed** themselves. That's why they practice hunting early on in their lives. This survival education also extends to animals that live in groups. Baby monkeys, for example, will spend as much as half their waking hours playing. They are learning not only how to win and lose make-believe fights and games but also how to get along with other group members. So, the next time you see young animals playing, remember that they are actually gaining valuable social **skills** and behavior that will keep them safe in the future, and not just having fun.

Vocabulary Study

A Choose and write the correct word.

> feed   strengthen   domestic   obvious   skills

1. It's important to have many ___________ when applying for a job.

2. Lana needs to ___________ her golf skills before she enters her fist tournament.

3. I ________ my animals twice a day, once in the morning and once at night.

4. ___________ animals are not so easy to raise.

5. The president said it is ___________ that our economy is suffering from high oil prices.

B Replace the underlined words with a synonym from the box.

> escape   predator   extends   young   cute

1. My friend Steve has a really <u>adorable</u> cat.

2. Even a <u>marauder</u> like a lion needs to play.

3. The new character will <u>broaden</u> its appeal.

4. Tommy wanted to <u>flee</u> from the scary monsters.

5. The <u>babies</u> of animals need to play.

Main idea

This story is about _____________.

   a. cats and dogs   b. group behavior

   c. animals playing   d. feeding animals

03

Paragraph Understanding

Choose the correct answer.

1. Paragraph ____   Playing also teaches animals important social skills.
2. Paragraph ____   Predators like lions and wolves practice hunting when they are young.
3. Paragraph ____   Animals are going to a kind of "school" when they play.
4. Paragraph ____   Learning to play when young can be the difference between living and dying for animals.

Looking for detail

Circle the correct answer.

1. What does playing NOT teach animals when they are young?
   a. Survival skills
   b. How to eat properly
   c. Balance and muscle control
   d. Social skills

2. For animals, playing is a form of ___________ .
   a. military training
   b. punishment
   c. education
   d. dietary exercise

3. Which paragraph talks about how playing helps animals deal with others?
   a. Paragraph 1
   b. Paragraph 2
   c. Paragraph 3
   d. Paragraph 4

4. It's also important for human beings to ___________ .
   a. eat a lot of food
   b. own many pets
   c. play when they are young
   d. learn how to play like an animal

Developing Skills

Find a grammatical mistake and correct it.

1. I had a pet since I was ten.

   ____

2. Behavior learns as a youngster can save an animal as an adult.

   ____

3. Playing is vital for animals that lives in groups.

   ____

4. Denise loves watching monkeys to play in the zoo.

   ____

5. Even cute animals need to play when been young.

   ____

T6   Summary & Listening Practice

Read the paragraph and fill in as many blanks as you can.
Then listen to the recording and fill in the rest of the blanks.

Animals look very ① ___________ when they are playing. But it's very important for them to play when they are young because it teaches them vital ② ___________ and behavior that they will need as adults. It is especially important for animals in the wild, as it can be the difference between life and ③ ___________. In addition, it teaches them how to get ④ ___________ with other animals in a group. Thus the next time you see an animal ⑤ ___________, you will now understand the reason why they are doing so.

04   The Story of the White House

1. Who was the first President to live in the White House?
2. What was the first disaster that the White House faced?
3. Can you name some pets that children of U.S. Presidents have kept?

 T7

1   Did you ever wonder how the White House got its name? This famous building — home to the American President — had a very interesting beginning. **Construction** on what was called the "President's House" began in 1792, after a plan for its building was chosen that same year. President John Adams and his wife, Abigail, moved in to their new home in 1800, though the home was far from complete. Out front, the unfinished lawn was nothing but mud, and many rooms weren't even ready to be lived in. In fact, Abigail Adams had to dry her laundry inside the White House, in the East Room!

2   But it was only during this first decade of the 1800's that the building became known as the White House. Before that, it was called the President's House or President's Palace. During the War of 1812, the White House experienced its first **disaster**. The British set fire to it in 1814. Fortunately, the outside walls of the White House were saved by a **violent** thunderstorm, and it was rebuilt, repainted, and ready to house another First Family. Except for the country's very first President, George Washington, every American President has lived and worked in the White House. Since those early years, it has become an important **symbol** of democracy and the United States.

3   Another interesting fact **concerns** the children of American Presidents. Over the years, they have done many funny things while living there. For instance, Abraham Lincoln's son Tad accidentally blasted open a door with his toy cannon. In addition, all kinds of pets have been kept there, from a goat to a bear to snakes. Teddy Roosevelt's children even moved their pony from floor to floor by using the White House's elevator. Sheep were once used to "cut" the lawn, but no longer.

4   Despite all these changes, the White House has remained the home of the American President, ever since it was first occupied by a First Family in 1800. With 132 rooms, it is an amazing architectural building with a long and interesting history.

Vocabulary Study

A Choose and write the correct word.

| symbol | disaster | concerns | construction | violent |

1. The eagle is an important ___________ in the United States.

2. There were ___________ protests downtown, leaving many people injured.

3. An earthquake is a natural ___________.

4. The ___________ work requires a lot of resources.

5. This book ___________ the development of character.

B Replace the underlined words with a synonym from the box.

| laundry | blasted | unfinished | complete | occupied |

1. The movie was a <u>perfect</u> success.

2. We usually hang our <u>wash</u> out in the backyard.

3. The painting was <u>incomplete</u>.

4. The helicopter <u>smashed</u> the wall.

5. The land was <u>inhabited</u> by Native Americans.

Main idea

This story is about the ______________.
a. American President's home   b. American wars
c. history of the U.S.   d. white buildings

Paragraph Understanding

Choose the correct answer.

1. Paragraph ___   Even when President Adams moved in to the White House, it was not completely finished.
2. Paragraph ___   The White House has changed a lot over the years.
3. Paragraph ___   Every American president has lived and worked from the White House except one.
4. Paragraph ___   Children have their own interesting history at the White House.

Looking for detail

Circle the correct answer.

1. What happened to the White House during the War of 1812?
   - a. John and Abigail Adams moved in.
   - b. It was finally completed.
   - c. It was burned down.
   - d. It was hit by lightening.

2. Theodore Roosevelt's kids moved their pony around the White House __________.
   - a. by truck
   - b. by riding it
   - c. by pulleys and leavers
   - d. by elevator

3. Which paragraph talks about children who have lived at the White House?
   - a. Paragraph 1
   - b. Paragraph 2
   - c. Paragraph 3
   - d. Paragraph 4

4. Before 1800, George Washington __________.
   - a. was not President
   - b. lived somewhere besides the White House
   - c. did not fight in any wars
   - d. and John Adams were good friends

Developing Skills

Find a grammatical mistake and correct it.

1. Abigail Adams was used to dry the wash inside the White House.

   ____

2. My dream is to visiting Washington D.C. one day.

   ____

3. There were many changes since the White House was first occupied in 1800.

   ____

4. The White House has becoming an important symbol in the United States.

   ____

5. The White House got its name after it was painting white.

   ____

 T8 ### Summary & Listening Practice

Read the paragraph and fill in as many blanks as you can.
Then listen to the recording and fill in the rest of the blanks.

The White House has a very interesting ① __________. John Adams and his wife, Abigail, were the first residents of the White House. However, even when they moved in, it was far from ② __________. The British ③ __________ fire to the White House in the 19th century, but the damages were quickly ④ __________. Part of the unique story about the White House ⑤ __________ the pets that Presidents' children have kept there. Today, the White House is one of the most famous homes in the world.

Pre-reading activity
1. What is alchemy?
2. What were the ancient world's four basic elements?
3. Which branch of science did alchemy help establish?

 T9

1 Much of what we use in everyday life is due to the magic of chemistry. In the past, in nations and **empires** all over the world, many people had tried to change lead and other common metals into gold and silver. But it was very difficult. For more than a millennium, these people — some of them were real scientists and some just creative entrepreneurs — practiced a mixture of magic, science, and religion. This came to be known as "alchemy."

2 Back in the ancient world, people believed that everything was **composed** of four basic substances — fire, air, earth, and water. They thought that if you heated, cooled or dried any substance, it would change into one of these basic elements of Mother Nature. Alchemists, on the other hand, discovered something new. One could **transform** one substance into another substance by changing the balance of the four elements. They even thought it might be possible that the color, shine, and texture of gold could be transferred to other metals.

3 Part of the reason that people wanted to learn how to make gold is that it **lasts** such a long time. Others thought that a successful alchemist held the key to **prolonging** one's life. In order to keep their secrets safe, alchemists used to write in code, so nobody could understand what they wrote.

4 No one has ever successfully changed lead into gold. In the past, there were some alchemists who misled people into thinking this was possible. They basically tricked people. One trick was for an alchemist to use a container with a wax bottom, under which was hidden some pieces of gold. After the container was heated, the wax would melt and the gold would mix in with the lead. Those watching would be amazed, so they would pay the alchemist to "make" more gold. Although alchemists failed to turn lead into gold, they did make one lasting contribution. Their work led to what is now referred to as modern chemistry.

Vocabulary Study

A Choose and write the correct word.

> lasts   transform   empires   composed   prolonging

1. The professor gave her students more time by ____________ the deadline.

2. This light bulb ____________ up to 1,000 hours.

3. Water is ____________ of hydrogen and oxygen.

4. The plan helped ____________ the area into a tourist attraction.

5. There were many ____________ in the ancient world.

B Replace the underlined words with a synonym from the box.

> substance   entrepreneur   code   mixture   amazed

1. The message was written in cipher.

2. Many people were astounded by the results.

3. Water is a vital ingredient in beer.

4. My sister really wants to be a businessperson.

5. The pain is a combination of different feelings.

Main idea

This story is about ____________.

    a. magic   b. alchemy

    c. gold and silver   d. chemistry

Paragraph Understanding

Choose the correct answer.

1. Paragraph ___   Long ago, people believed everything in the world was made up of four substances.
2. Paragraph ___   Alchemy is a mixture of magic, science, and religion.
3. Paragraph ___   Alchemy was seen as important because it was the key to living forever.
4. Paragraph ___   Some alchemists used to fool people into believing they could really change lead into gold.

Looking for detail

Circle the correct answer.

1. Which of the following was not considered one of the four basic elements of the world long ago?
   a. Fire
   b. Gold
   c. Air
   d. Water

2. To keep their secrets safe, alchemists used to write in ___________.
   a. black ink
   b. foreign languages
   c. pen
   d. code

3. Which paragraph talks about a specific trick alchemists played on people?
   a. Paragraph 1
   b. Paragraph 2
   c. Paragraph 3
   d. Paragraph 4

4. Alchemy led to a better understanding of ___________.
   a. science
   b. religion
   c. magic
   d. business

Developing Skills

Find a grammatical mistake and correct it.

1. People who wanted to live forever were interesting in alchemy.

____

2. Some businesspeople can be very dishonestly.

____

3. I wish I can turned lead into gold.

____

4. People across the earth were fascinate by alchemy in the past.

____

5. We should thankful alchemists for our understanding of chemistry.

____

T 10   Summary & Listening Practice

Read the paragraph and fill in as many blanks as you can.
Then listen to the recording and fill in the rest of the blanks.

Many people wanted to ① ____________ lead into gold and silver in the past. In the ancient world, it was believed that everything was composed of four basic ② ____________. Alchemists felt they could ③ ____________ one substance into another substance by changing the balance of the four elements. Alchemy was thought to be the key to ④ ____________ life. Although no one has ⑤ ____________ successfully turned lead into gold, alchemy did lead to modern chemistry.

06   A Great Inventor

 T11

1. Talking on the phone is a daily activity that we all take for **granted**, whether it is a modern cell phone or just an ordinary house phone. Of course, the telephone began with Alexander Graham Bell's marvelous invention over a hundred years ago. From a young age, Bell was interested in science. But he invented much more than just the telephone. His passion for science grew after his mother became deaf.

2. He **desperately** wanted to help those who did not have the ability to hear. So, while he taught deaf children during the day, Bell would often stay up late conducting experiments with electricity. Even though the telegraph had been used to send messages along a wire long before Bell was born, he was the first to realize that a human voice could also be carried over wires. In 1877, in Salem, Massachusetts, Bell called his **assistant**, Thomas Watson, who was in Boston, 16 miles away. Watson read a news story and sang a song for Bell, who listened to it in a room full of people.

3. The same technology used to make the telephone eventually helped Bell make a machine that could tell whether someone had trouble hearing or not. People listened for high and low sounds by wearing earphones. Yet Bell invented more than just those two things. He also invented a metal **detector**, which was very useful for doctors to find a **bullet** inside patients suffering from gunshot wounds. When doctors used Bell's new device, it would beep whenever it got near a piece of metal, or a bullet as the case might be.

4. Additionally, Bell also invented a new kind of boat motor, a way to build stronger homes and a machine to help people breathe. Alexander Graham Bell was continually inventing things until the day he died. When someone once asked him how he had the time to invent so many things, he responded, "A true inventor can't help inventing any more than he can help thinking."

Vocabulary Study

A Choose and write the correct word.

> granted   desperately   assistant   detector   bullet

1. The man was shot several times, but was not hit by a single ___________ .

2. People take their health for ___________ .

3. A special ___________ is used to identify dangerous materials.

4. Thanks to her exceptional ___________ , Marie could do many things.

5. Clean air is ___________ needed.

B Replace the underlined words with a synonym from the box.

> invent   conducted   experiments   modern   device

1. The scientist <u>performed</u> many tests.

2. She is familiar with <u>contemporary</u> literature.

3. An MP3 player is a convenient <u>gadget</u>.

4. Not many people can <u>contrive</u> new things.

5. Mrs. Smith carried out the <u>tests</u>.

Main idea

This story is about ___________ .

  a. an inventor   b. a famous bell
  c. inventions   d. the telephone

Paragraph Understanding

Choose the correct answer.

1. Paragraph ___   Bell was interested in helping the deaf.
2. Paragraph ___   Bell's metal detector helped doctors save the lives of gunshot victims.
3. Paragraph ___   In 1877, Bell listened to his assistant sing a song and read a news story over the telephone.
4. Paragraph ___   Always full of energy, Bell said a true inventor never stops inventing.

Looking for detail

Circle the correct answer.

1. What did Alexander Graham Bell do to help deaf people early in his life?
   a. He taught them.
   b. He built them telephones.
   c. He sang to them.
   d. He did experiments with them.

2. Metal detectors helped doctors find bullets inside patients by ________.
   a. exploding near metal
   b. eating any metal it found
   c. beeping around pieces of metal
   d. making metal disappear

3. Which paragraph talks about an invention of Bell's that helped people breathe?
   a. Paragraph 1
   b. Paragraph 2
   c. Paragraph 3
   d. Paragraph 4

4. Although some people think that Bell invented only the telephone, __________.
   a. he was actually deaf
   b. they are probably right
   c. in fact he invented much more
   d. no one remembers his other inventions

Developing Skills

Find a grammatical mistake and correct it.

1. Alexander Graham Bell was not deaf, but his mother is.

____

2. I think the telephone was an important invent.

____

3. Today, Bell serves like a role model for future inventors and scientists.

____

4. A form of Bell's metal detector is still in used at airports.

____

5. We should to make Inventors' Day a public holiday.

____

T 12   Summary & Listening Practice

**Read the paragraph and fill in as many blanks as you can.
Then listen to the recording and fill in the rest of the blanks.**

From a young age, Alexander Graham Bell was passionate about ① ___________ . Bell was interested in helping people who were deaf, as his mother did not have the ② ___________ to hear. Bell's most famous ③ ___________ was the telephone. However, he also invented a ④ ___________ detector, a new type of boat motor, a way to build stronger homes, and a machine to help people breathe. When asked how he could work so hard and invent so many things, Bell replied that a ⑤ ___________ inventor never stops inventing.

07 JAPANESE AMERICANS IN WORLD WAR II

 T 13

1 The morning of December 7, 1941 started out no differently than any other for six-year old Jeanne Wakatsuki and her sisters. The girls, who were standing near the coast of Long Beach, California, watched as their father's fishing boat went out to sea. Almost immediately, the boat returned right away. As their father's boat was coming back, someone on the deck yelled out, "The Japanese have bombed Pearl Harbor!" America was now at war with Japan.

2 For Jeanne's father, Mr. Wakatsuki, who was born in Japan, this turn of events would have disastrous consequences. At the **outbreak** of the war, other Americans began to **distrust** Japanese Americans. Even though his children were born in the United States, Mr. Wakatsuki's family would suffer because he was Japanese. Very soon after the start of the war, the U.S. government took away the homes, businesses, and possessions of thousands of Japanese Americans even though many of these families thought of themselves as true Americans. The government sent all Japanese Americans to internment camps — a type of **detention** facility. For the Wakatsukis, they ended up in the Sierra Nevada Mountains in a camp called Manzanar.

3 In the beginning, the Manzanar camp was poorly furnished and had little equipment. Over time, the Japanese Americans who were interred there built things like schools and rock gardens. Like many other children, Jeanne Wakatsuki would hike in the high, chilly California mountains. However, because they were seen as **enemies** of the country, no one was allowed to leave the camp for three years.

4 Years later, in 2004, Jeanne Wakatsuki wrote a book about her experiences at Manzanar. By the time it was published, the American government had realized its dreadful mistake. It had been many decades after the war. The government decided to **compensate** the Japanese American victims with money. Yet the truth is that no amount of money could make up for the lost years that were stolen from loyal American citizens like Jeanne Wakatsuki and her family.

Vocabulary Study

A Choose and write the correct word.

> outbreak   enemies   detention   distrust   compensated

1. The two groups couldn't agree because there was ___________ on both sides.

2. The workers were ___________ after being fired illegally from their jobs.

3. The ___________ of the disease was not foreseen.

4. He was held in ___________ for ten years.

5. Paul is so kind and friendly that he has no ___________.

B Replace the underlined words with a synonym from the box.

> stolen   immediately   built   loyal   dreadful

1. We were shocked at the outrageous mistake.

2. All the king's men were faithful to him.

3. Victory is not achieved instantly.

4. The Empire State Building was constructed last century.

5. We had everything taken from us at the beach.

Main idea

This story is about _______________.
   a. Japanese camps in America   b. Japanese American internment
   c. Japanese Americans   d. World War II

Paragraph Understanding

Choose the correct answer.

1. Paragraph ___   Jeanne Wakatsuki and her family were not allowed to leave Manzanar for three years.
2. Paragraph ___   The Japanese bombed Pearl Harbor on Dec. 7, 1941.
3. Paragraph ___   Sometime afterward, Jeanne Wakatsuki wrote a book about her time at Manzanar.
4. Paragraph ___   After America declared war on Japan, Japanese Americans were sent to interment camps.

Looking for detail

Circle the correct answer.

1. When did Japanese Americans have all their possessions taken from them?
   a. After they were interned.
   b. After they landed in America.
   c. After the end of World War II.
   d. After America declared war on Japan.

2. One of the first things people built at Manzanar were ___________.
   a. factories   b. schools
   c. shelters   d. cemeteries

3. Which paragraph talks about what Jeanne Wakatsuki's father did?
   a. Paragraph 1   b. Paragraph 2
   c. Paragraph 3   d. Paragraph 4

4. We know more about the conditions at Manzanar because of ___________.
   a. World War II
   b. Jeanne Wakatsuki's book
   c. Jeanne Wakatsuki's father
   d. Japanese Americans who moved back to Japan

Developing Skills

Find a grammatical mistake and correct it.

1. Americans distrusted Japanese Americans while World War II.

   ____

2. Many monuments have been built to honor people what died in internment camps.

   ____

3. I enjoy to learn about American history.

   ____

4. A girl calling Sally read Jeanne Wakatsuki's book.

   ____

5. Japanese Americans were compensate only a little after the war.

   ____

T14   Summary & Listening Practice

Read the paragraph and fill in as many blanks as you can.
Then listen to the recording and fill in the rest of the blanks.

America ① ____________ war on Japan after the Asian country bombed Pearl Harbor in 1941. Soon after this, Jeanne Wakatsuki's family, along with all Japanese Americans, had their ② ____________ taken from them. They were then ③ ____________ to internment camps, where they were unable to leave for three years. Jeanne Wakatsuki and her ④ ____________ were sent to a camp called Manzanar in the Sierra Nevada Mountains. Years later, Japanese Americans received ⑤ ____________ for their time in internment camps, and Jeanne Wakatsuki published a book in 2004 about her experiences at Manzanar.

Pre-reading activity

1. Where have the San traditionally lived?
2. How do the San catch big animals?
3. What is happening to the San today?

1. Of all the desolate and dry places in the world, the African desert must be one of the toughest to survive in. The Kalahari Desert has very little water, food or **shelter**. Even though many people could not live in such surroundings, one group has managed to do so for centuries. They are called the San and have thrived for generations.

2. To survive in the Kalahari, the San need to use special skills. One thing they need to do every day is protect their skin from the powerful sun **overhead**. They accomplish this by rubbing oil on their skin. Dust from the desert sticks to the oil and blocks out the sun's **rays**. The San also have other inventive ways of living in such a dry climate. To find water, they will plunge a long, hollow reed into the ground and then suck on it. This slowly draws the water up from below the ground. If they have any extra water, they will store it in empty ostrich eggs. Then they will bury the eggs underground to make sure the sun doesn't dry them out.

3. What is most amazing is the San's ability to find food. While the women are out looking for wild potatoes, roots and fruits, the men can actually hunt a day's worth of food in about two hours. When they want to eat meat, the **skilled** San will find small desert creatures like lizards and insects. But they are not averse to hunting larger animals. The men often go after larger game after camouflaging themselves in leaves and feathers. With these "outfits," they creep up close to the animal and kill it with poison-tipped arrows. While the meat is obviously eaten, the skin is used for clothing and the stomach is made into a water bag. No part of an animal is ever wasted.

4. Eventually, however, modern **technology** has changed life for many of the San. Despite living in the remote Kalahari, the conveniences of modern life have slowly come to influence the San. Some have had their land taken from them. Still others have moved to more settled areas. Today there are still a few San living the traditional lifestyle in the desert.

Vocabulary Study

A Choose and write the correct word.

overhead	technology	shelter	skilled	rays

1. The factory employs only a few ___________ workers.

2. Everyone agrees that ___________ makes life more convenient.

3. The moon's ___________ were a beautiful bluish color last night.

4. The sun was very high ___________ in the sky yesterday.

5. When camping, it's helpful to find a dry place to build your ___________.

B Replace the underlined words with a synonym from the box.

store	looking	changed	protect	hollow

1. The teacher <u>altered</u> the test this year.

2. The animals went <u>searching</u> for food in the forest.

3. A squirrel lived inside the <u>empty</u> tree trunk.

4. Just <u>deposit</u> it in the fridge.

5. You should <u>shield</u> your eyes from the sun.

Main idea

This story is about ______________.

   a. deserts of the world   b. African tribes

   c. an African desert   d. a desert tribe

Paragraph Understanding

Choose the correct answer.

1. Paragraph ___   Though life has changed for many of the San, some still live in the traditional way.
2. Paragraph ___   When they catch a big animal, no part of it is ever wasted.
3. Paragraph ___   To protect their skin, the San rub oil on their skin.
4. Paragraph ___   The San of the Kalahari Desert have lived there for hundreds of years.

Looking for detail

Circle the correct answer.

1. What does oil on the San's skin do to protect it from the sun?
   a. Water sticks to it.
   b. It attracts the sun's rays.
   c. It softens their skin.
   d. Dust sticks to it.

2. The San will use the stomach of a large animal to make ___________.
   a. food
   b. shelter
   c. a water bag
   d. clothes

3. Which paragraph talks about how the San gather water?
   a. Paragraph 1
   b. Paragraph 2
   c. Paragraph 3
   d. Paragraph 4

4. For the San who still live in the Kalahari Desert, they probably don't use ___________.
   a. much oil on their skin
   b. their skills anymore
   c. much modern technology
   d. hollow reeds anymore

Developing Skills

Find a grammatical mistake and correct it.

1. I have seen a movie about the San of the Kalahari Desert last night.

2. The way the San live is very impressed.

3. It's amazing which their skin doesn't burn under the desert sun's rays.

4. It is easy to understand why have some San moved to cities.

5. It would be a fun to travel to the Kalahari Desert for a short trip.

T 16   Summary & Listening Practice

Read the paragraph and fill in as many blanks as you can. Then listen to the recording and fill in the rest of the blanks.

One of the toughest places for people to live in the world is the Kalahari Desert of Africa. However, the San have thrived there for ① ___________. They need special ② ___________ to survive, though. They need to be creative in ③ ___________ their skin, finding water, and catching animals for food. Modern ④ ___________ has led many of the San to move to urban centers, but some continue to live the traditional ⑤ ___________ in the Kalahari Desert.

Pre-reading activity

1. How many classes are there when classifying stones?
2. What grade rocks are most common in nature?
3. What is the strongest mineral on Earth?

 T 17

1. Most people never pay attention to ordinary rocks. But geologists — the scientists who study rocks — are so fascinated by the size, shape, and tone of rocks that they have their own classification system. Rocks can be graded, from Class One to Class Ten. Geology experts place a rock into one of 10 classes after determining how hard it is. Most rocks you find fall somewhere in the first seven classes of rocks. For a lucky few, you might find a rock that falls into one of the top three classes. These are called **precious** gemstones.

2. Fortunately, you don't need any fancy **equipment** to test a rock for its hardness. Your fingernail is perfect for scratching many of the softer rocks. If the rock you find is strong enough to make a scratch on talc, then it is a Class One soft stone. Class Two rocks can also be **scratched** with your fingernail. To scratch a Class Three stone you'll need a penny, as it will scratch minerals like calcite. To scratch a rock in Class Four or Five, you'll need a knife. A steel file is needed for rocks that are Class Six.

3. In Class Seven, rocks contain quartz, one of the hardest and most common minerals found anywhere. Although it can scratch all rocks from Class One to Class Six, it can't scratch topaz and other gemstones of Class Eight. It takes a Class Nine sapphire to scratch topaz.

4. Finally, the only **mineral** that can scratch Class Nine stones is a diamond. It is the only Class Ten stone. That's because diamonds are so hard that they can cut through just about anything. In fact, they are even used to drill oil wells and underground tunnels! If you ask what natural **object** on Earth can scratch a diamond, well the answer is ... another diamond.

Vocabulary Study

A Choose and write the correct word.

scratched	object	mineral	precious	equipment

1. Canada is rich in ___________ mines.

2. You need a lot of ___________ to play ice hockey.

3. My mother's wedding ring is my most ___________ possession.

4. I ___________ my knee when I fell down on the pavement.

5. The man had an ___________ inside his jacket which I couldn't see.

B Replace the underlined words with a synonym from the box.

contains	fancy	classified	ordinary	experts

1. The movie <u>encompasses</u> many subjects.

2. Many <u>specialists</u> were concerned about the situation.

3. There is nothing <u>special</u> about my umbrella.

4. Diamonds can be <u>separated</u> into some categories.

5. The girl caught a very <u>commonplace</u> sickness

Main idea

This story is about ______________
   a. grading stones
   b. making stones
   c. finding stones
   d. selling stones

Paragraph Understanding

Choose the correct answer.

1. Paragraph ____   For Class One to Class Six rocks, you don't need any special equipment to test for hardness.

2. Paragraph ____   To scratch a rock from Class Seven to Nine, you'll need a special mineral.

3. Paragraph ____   Experts classify rocks and stones into one of ten classes.

4. Paragraph ____   The only mineral in Class Ten is a diamond.

Looking for detail

Circle the correct answer.

1. What is the material in Class Seven rocks that can scratch any lower class rock?
   a. Sapphire   b. Quartz
   c. Calcite   d. Diamond

2. A mineral's class depends on its ____________.
   a. hardness   b. cost
   c. value   d. rarity

3. Which paragraph talks about what is the world's toughest mineral?
   a. Paragraph 1   b. Paragraph 2
   c. Paragraph 3   d. Paragraph 4

4. The only substance that a sapphire cannot scratch is ____________.
   a. diamond   b. quartz
   c. topaz   d. talc

Developing Skills

Find a grammatical mistake and correct it.

1. I have found a wallet yesterday.

   ____

2. Mom has a beautiful diamond necklaces.

   ____

3. Diamond cutters are a piece of special equipments.

   ____

4. Precious gems are expensive to purchase them.

   ____

5. Everybody have a right to be happy.

   ____

T 18　Summary & Listening Practice

Read the paragraph and fill in as many blanks as you can.
Then listen to the recording and fill in the rest of the blanks.

Rocks and stones can be separated into classes depending on their
① _____________. Class One rocks are the easiest to ② _____________, and Class
Ten are the most difficult. In fact, to classify rocks as Class One to Class Six,
all you need is a penny or pocketknife to scratch most of their
③ _____________. Rocks in Class Seven have
quartz in them, but those in Class Eight and
Nine have even harder surfaces. The last
three classes are called ④ _____________
gemstones, with the hardest stone in the
world being a ⑤ _____________.

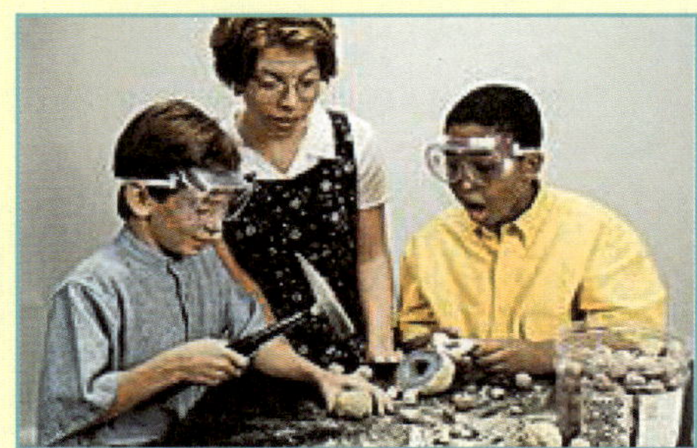

10 All about Helicopters

1. How do airplanes fly?
2. How does helicopters fly?
3. How many levers does a helicopter pilot usually have to control at once?

 T 19

1   They are used as military vehicles by the army, as air ambulances by hospitals, and for traffic reports by radio and TV stations. There are big ones and little ones. Both the military and **civilians** can use them. What are they? Yes, they're helicopters. We've all seen a helicopter before, either in person or on TV, but have you ever wondered how it stays up in the air? Well, no matter what type of helicopter it is, the same **principle** of physics explains why it stays aloft.

2   Airplanes, as you might know, fly because of something called "lift." Air flows more quickly over the top of their wings because they're curved. With less air pressure on the top, and with the air pressure remaining **stable** under the wing, the airplane is forced up, meaning it flies. A helicopter works in the same way. It might not have wings that look exactly like those of an airplane, but it does have rotor blades on its roof. These blades are curved and basically function like an airplane wing. Air is forced over the wings as the blades rotate and lift is created.

3   Inside the helicopter, the pilot uses three levers to **steer**. One lever makes the helicopter go up or down by changing the angle of the rotor blades. If the helicopter needs to stay in one place — called hovering — this same lever is used. The pilot can use the second lever to make the helicopter go forward, backward, or sideways. Finally, the small blades on the back of the helicopter are controlled by the third lever. It takes an amazingly skilled pilot to move all three levers at once to change directions.

4   It's easy to understand why flying a helicopter is such a difficult job. In fact, many pilots compare flying a helicopter to sitting on a really big rubber ball that keeps trying to tip over. It takes great skill and concentration to successfully control a helicopter. Fortunately, though, any certified pilot always does his or her best to **ensure** that every trip up in a helicopter is a safe one.

Vocabulary Study

A Choose and write the correct word.

| principle | ensure | steer | civilians | stable |

1. The ___________ of relativity is difficult to understand.

2. Do your best to ___________ everyone enjoys themselves.

3. The helicopter is ___________ now, but it was bouncing before.

4. It's easier to ___________ a car than a helicopter.

5. The terrorist attack left eight ___________ dead.

B Replace the underlined words with a synonym from the box.

| aloft | amazingly | concentration | basically | certified |

1. <u>Attentiveness</u> is the key to success.

2. Try to hold the paper airplane <u>up in the air</u>.

3. They are <u>essentially</u> the same.

4. <u>Incredibly</u>, nobody was hurt in the accident.

5. Amy is a <u>licensed</u> nurse.

Main idea

This story is about ______________.
   a. the effect of air on helicopters   b. how helicopters fly
   c. steering a helicopter   d. objects that fly

Paragraph Understanding

Choose the correct answer.

1. Paragraph ____   There are many different kinds of helicopters.
2. Paragraph ____   Although flying a helicopter is difficult, pilots always do their best to make sure every flight is a safe one.
3. Paragraph ____   A helicopter pilot often has to steer with three levers at one time.
4. Paragraph ____   Airplanes and helicopters both stay up in the air because of lift.

Looking for detail

Circle the correct answer.

1. What is it called when the helicopter stays in one place?
   - a. leverage
   - b. hovering
   - c. flying
   - d. steering

2. With airplanes, air flows quicker ____________.
   - a. around the tail of the plane
   - b. over the surface of the plane
   - c. under the wings
   - d. over the top of wings

3. Which paragraph talks about steering a helicopter?
   - a. Paragraph 1
   - b. Paragraph 2
   - c. Paragraph 3
   - d. Paragraph 4

4. Sometimes a helicopter pilot has to use all three levers at the same time just to ____________.
   - a. lift off
   - b. land
   - c. hover
   - d. change directions

Developing Skills

Find a grammatical mistake and correct it.

1. Have you ever flied in a helicopter before.

   ____

2. To steering a helicopter must require a lot of training.

   ____

3. It's still hard of me to understand how an airpplane stays in the air.

   ____

4. I'm afraid of get into a helicopter.

   ____

5. One of my favorite TV show is about a helicopter pilot.

   ____

 T20   ## Summary & Listening Practice

Read the paragraph and fill in as many blanks as you can.
Then listen to the recording and fill in the rest of the blanks.

Most people are aware that there are many different types of ① ___________.
Interestingly, airplanes and helicopters both fly using the same ② ___________, and that is called *lift*. An airplane uses its wings, while a helicopter uses its rotor

③ ___________. Flying a helicopter is not an easy job. Often the pilot will have to steer with three ④ ___________ at once. It might be tough to fly a helicopter, but pilots do their best to ⑤ ___________ that every flight is a safe one.

11 *Native American Kachinas*

 T21

1. Native Americans have a long and **illustrious** tradition. **Central** to many native cultures are spirits, some of which are called kachinas. Specifically, the Hopi, a Native American tribe, believe that these spirits are directly connected with the four seasons of the year. In the months when the weather is cold, kachinas will retreat to the faraway mountains. But as spring gives way to warmer weather, the kachinas return and live among the Hopi people during the growing season.

2. During the warm months, the Hopi celebrate with many festivals. The spirits' importance is recognized by including them in these festivals. The men of the tribe put on masks and costumes to represent the kachinas. These take many forms — some in the shape of clowns, demons, and animals. Each of the 250 different kachinas has its own unique personality and role.

3. A planting **ceremony** called *Powamu* begins the year's festivities in February. During this time, the Crow Mother kachina gives gifts and sprouting beans to the Hopi. The last ceremony of the year takes place in July, when the Home Dance — or Niman — is performed. Through the ceremony, the kachinas are all preparing to go back to their mountain homes.

4. It's not just adults that play a role in representing kachinas, though. Children are also expected to learn the roles of the spirits. Adults help the children by **carving** kachina dolls, each one decorated as a **specific** spirit. This is a very creative time for all. When they are completed, they are hung on the walls of homes so that kachina dolls can help children think of their culture.

Vocabulary Study

A Choose and write the correct word.

> ceremony   specific   illustrious   central   carving

1. The children are all ____________ things out of wood.

2. Exercise is ____________ to your health.

3. I don't have any ____________ goals for my future.

4. Peter enjoyed a[n] ____________ career.

5. The awards ____________ is taking place at the City Hotel.

B Replace the underlined words with a synonym from the box.

> includes   tribes   retreated   recognized   specifically

1. Their efforts were <u>acknowledged</u> by the public.

2. They <u>withdrew</u> to the living room.

3. <u>In particular</u>, Michele and Michael can't come.

4. The ceremony <u>embraces</u> many traditional elements.

5. There are many different Native American <u>groups</u>.

Main idea

This story is about ________________
- a. Native American spirits
- b. Native Americans
- c. A Native American tribe
- d. Spirits of North America

Paragraph Understanding

Choose the correct answer.

1. Paragraph ___ The Hopi celebrate the spirits by holding festivals in their honor.
2. Paragraph ___ Kachina ceremonies take place from February to July every year.
3. Paragraph ___ Kachinas are especially relevant to the Hopi.
4. Paragraph ___ Children are expected to play a role in representing kachinas, too.

Looking for detail

Circle the correct answer.

1. The Hopi believe the spirits are connected with the ___________.
   a. ghosts
   b. seasons
   c. mountains
   d. sun

2. What are the spirits preparing for in Niman?
   a. To go home
   b. To fall asleep
   c. To plant crops
   d. To attend a festival

3. Which paragraph talks about the role of children with kachinas?
   a. Paragraph 1
   b. Paragraph 2
   c. Paragraph 3
   d. Paragraph 4

4. Kachinas still play a role in Hopi culture in part because ___________.
   a. the children carve masks
   b. they are kind and generous
   c. the women wear costumes
   d. they live in the mountains

Developing Skills

Rearrange the words below to make correct sentences.

1. students   learn   all   literature   about   should

   ____

2. important   Americans   to   spirits   Native   are

   ____

3. is   February   ceremony   in   held   the

   ____

4. can   fun   masks   be   carving

   ____

5. would   attend   we   like   festival   to   the

   ____

T 22   Summary & Listening Practice

**Read the paragraph and fill in as many blanks as you can.
Then listen to the recording and fill in the rest of the blanks.**

Kachinas are ① ____________ to all Native
Americans, though they are ② ____________
special to the Hopi. The Hopi celebrate the
③ ____________ weather by holding several
festivals from February to July every year. At
these ④ ____________, the men wear masks and
costumes that represent the 250 different
kachinas. Children also play a role by
⑤ ____________ masks that are then hung on the
walls of their homes.

12   A Very Special Group of Islands

 T 23

1. Probably, there is no group of islands that is more unique than the Galapagos Islands off the coast of Ecuador. These volcanic islands in the Pacific Ocean were made famous by the naturalist Charles Darwin, but were originally discovered by sailors who nicknamed them the Enchanted Isles. Over hundreds and hundreds of years, the 13 Galapagos Islands became very unique because powerful storms brought many different species of animals to their shores.

2. Over time, many new types of animals and birds **evolved**. As the animals had no way of getting off the islands — it was too far to swim or fly for many — they were forced to change their way of life. Adapting became necessary in order to survive. In one case, 13 kinds of finches — songbird — evolved out of one original species. One of them even learned how to use a twig to dig insects out of logs! Another kind of bird, the fish-eating cormorant, lost the use of its wings after it no longer needed them for flight. It learned to dive into the water where there were many fish.

3. Food was a key reason why many land animals, like the lizard, also had to change their habits. After realizing that there wasn't enough food on land to allow it to survive, the lizard was forced to find its food in the water. Again, it was a case of **adapt** or die. Today it is the world's only lizard that feeds off the ocean. Another example is the giant tortoise, which used to **inhabit** every continent. Today, the Galapagos Islands are the only place where you can find this magnificent creature. On one of the islands, these giant tortoises grew **exceptionally** long necks because there was not much ground food. By growing a longer neck it was able to reach up into the bushes for juicy leaves. As a matter of fact, the word galapagos means "tortoises" in Spanish.

4. The Galapagos Islands are a fascinating place to see Mother Nature at work. The islands are, in essence, a **miniature** biology laboratory. In addition, they have become a famous tourist destination and an important place for scientists and marine biologists to study.

Vocabulary Study

A Choose and write the correct word.

> adapt   evolved   inhabit   miniature   exceptionally

1. Martin Peters is a genius and an ___________ gifted piano player.

2. Human beings have ___________ over millions of years.

3. All animals have to ___________ to their environment.

4. Is childhood a ___________ version of adulthood?

5. Dinosaurs used to ___________ the earth.

B Replace the underlined words with a synonym from the box.

> originally   nicknamed   forced   fascinating   destination

1. The novel has an <u>intriguing</u> plot.

2. The building was <u>initially</u> constructed by the dock.

3. They were <u>coerced</u> to work for too many hours.

4. Success is not the <u>end point</u> of our lives.

5. Chris was <u>designated</u> as superb.

Main idea

This story is about ______________.
    a. evolutionary theory
    b. why the Galapagos Islands became a tourist destination
    c. the special nature of volcanic islands
    d. the uniqueness of the Galapagos Islands

Paragraph Understanding

Choose the correct answer.

1. Paragraph ____ Land animals also had to adapt to the conditions of the islands.
2. Paragraph ____ The islands are now a popular place for tourists and a unique laboratory for scientists.
3. Paragraph ____ A unique collection of islands, they are home to some special birds.
4. Paragraph ____ The Galapagos Islands were once called the Enchanted Isles.

Looking for detail

Circle the correct answer.

1. Who were the first people to visit the Galapagos Islands?
   - a. Tourists
   - b. Giant tortoises
   - c. Sailors
   - d. Scientists

2. Lizards adapted by ____________.
   - a. growing wings
   - b. finding food in water
   - c. learning how to use a twig
   - d. eating logs and wood

3. Which paragraph describes how birds adapted to life in the Galapagos Islands?
   - a. Paragraph 1
   - b. Paragraph 2
   - c. Paragraph 3
   - d. Paragraph 4

4. The first people to visit the Galapagos Islands were probably from ____________.
   - a. Brazil
   - b. America
   - c. Spain
   - d. Africa

Developing Skills

Rearrange the words below to make correct sentences.

1. the   Ecuador   aren't   Galapagos   Islands   far   from

   ____

2. adapted   many   animals   and   birds   to   there   life

   ____

3. on   looks   so   beautiful   the   islands   everything

   ____

4. picture   ever   have   you   tortoise   seen   a   of   a   giant

   ____

5. in   want   scientist   the   future   I   to   be   a

   ____

T24   Summary & Listening Practice

Read the paragraph and fill in as many blanks as you can.
Then listen to the recording and fill in the rest of the blanks.

Long ago, the Galapagos Islands were ① ___________ the Enchanted Isles by
visiting sailors. The 13 volcanic rocks that make up the chain of islands are
very special. They are not only home to land animals like the giant tortoise
that have ② ___________ to life there like
nowhere else on Earth, but are also home to
many ③ ___________ birds. Today, the islands
have become not only a famous tourist
④ ___________, but a popular place for
scientists and marine biologists to study
⑤ ___________.

13 *All That* JAZZ!

 T25

1   There is nothing like a bottle of red wine, good food and jazz music playing in the background. Early on in its history, jazz was played by African American musicians. It combined many different styles and traditions of music: American folk songs, religious gospel, and European classical music. It also incorporated **emotional** rhythms that slaves brought to America from West Africa centuries ago.

2   It might seem strange, but the first musicians who played jazz were poor and had little or no **conventional** music training. They played by ear because they weren't able to read sheet music. Instead of copying the stiff, formal sounds they heard, however, they adapted what they heard and **spontaneously** made their own music. They created a brand new sound, **improvising** what they heard from other music sources. As long as the notes didn't clash with the other people they were playing with, jazz musicians could play any notes they wanted to.

3   One of the most amazing parts of jazz is, and was, its tone. Jazz greats like Louis Armstrong and Jelly Roll Morton had the ability not only to **incorporate** Southern black speech into their music, but they also made their instruments sound like human voices.

4   Even today, most jazz songs start with a theme or a tune that listeners can easily recognize. A musician will begin by playing the song so that the audience has the tune in mind. After this, the melody or rhythm quickly changes as they play the piece again. Sometimes they can take just five or six notes and create a brand new song from it. The first jazz musicians didn't believe that their music shouldn't be written down, but these days almost everybody does. Jazz is always changing but never loses its roots.

Vocabulary Study

A Choose and write the correct word.

> incorporate improvise spontaneously emotional conventional

1. A good teacher should learn how to ___________ .

2. Koreans ___________ a lot of English into their language these days.

3. Amazingly, the audience responded ___________ .

4. The movie was so ___________ that nearly everyone cried.

5. ___________ wisdom is not always true.

B Replace the underlined words with a synonym from the box.

> combined   copy   stiff   theme   clash

1. The <u>subject</u> of the movie was eternal friendship.

2. It is illegal to <u>duplicate</u> the words of other writers.

3. Try not to <u>collide</u> with other vehicles on the road.

4. The work <u>blended</u> a variety of elements.

5. My legs felt so <u>rigid</u> that I couldn't go swimming.

Main idea

This story is about ______________ .
  a. jazz   b. Louis Armstrong
  c. human voices   d. African Americans

Paragraph Understanding

Choose the correct answer.

1. Paragraph ___   Jazz is a combination of many different types of music.
2. Paragraph ___   Great jazz musicians made their instruments sound like people's voices.
3. Paragraph ___   Although the music has changed, a theme or tune still starts off most jazz songs today.
4. Paragraph ___   Early jazz musicians didn't write down their music.

Looking for detail

Circle the correct answer.

1. Which of the following did not influence early jazz music?
   a. Religious music
   b. Classical music
   c. American folk songs
   d. Early rock and roll

2. One of the most amazing parts of early jazz was its ___________.
   a. popularity
   b. tone
   c. musicians
   d. loudness

3. Which paragraph talks about the blank speech of jazz?
   a. Paragraph 1
   b. Paragraph 2
   c. Paragraph 3
   d. Paragraph 4

4. Some of the first jazz musicians probably had no training because ___________.
   a. they didn't write down their music
   b. they couldn't read sheet music
   c. they had no money
   d. they had no talent

Developing Skills

Rearrange the words below to make correct sentences.

1. performer   favorite   My   is   Louis   jazz   Armstrong

   ____

2. spontaneous   the   musicians   the   were   really   at   concert

   ____

3. how   listen   on   do   you   to   music   the   radio   often

   ____

4. play   all   around   the   jazz   people   world   now

   ____

5. emotional   you   enjoy   listening   do   to   music

   ____

T26   Summary & Listening Practice

Read the paragraph and fill in as many blanks as you can.
Then listen to the recording and fill in the rest of the blanks.

Jazz was first ① ___________ by African Americans. It was a ② ___________ of many different types of music, from European classical music to West African slave rhythms. ③ ___________, jazz musicians didn't write down their music because they couldn't read sheet ④ ___________ or simply had very little training. Jazz musicians created a brand new sound with their songs and their instruments. Even today, jazz songs will still begin with a ⑤ ___________ or a tune that the musician can play around with.

 T 27

1. When a painting by Frida Kahlo was sold for $1.65 million in 1991, the price set a record for a work of art by a Latin American artist. Unlike some other famous European paintings which are **routinely auctioned** off for millions of dollars, Frida's painting is not particularly large or complicated. But it has amazingly bright colors that are appealing to the eye. In the painting, a Mexican woman with long hair, heavy eyebrows, and strong features appears to be staring directly into the viewer's eyes. This intense glare is what makes the painting so **appealing**.

2. Today, we know that the painting is a self-portrait of Frida Kahlo. But her life was not always a fun-filled one. She was badly injured in an accident as a teenager while growing up in Mexico. She spent a number of years in severe pain as she struggled to paint. When her **severely** broken body was placed in a rigid cast, Frida couldn't move any part of her body except her hands. This is the time she really began to paint.

3. Frida never recovered 100 percent from her injuries. Just as the pain lasted for much of her life, her passion to paint also was alive during most of her life. Despite all this hard work, Frida did not receive much recognition as an artist throughout her lifetime. At the time of her marriage, the public was more interested in the work of her husband, Diego Rivera.

4. Since her death in 1954, the art of Frida Kahlo has become better known in other parts of the world. But the highest **recognition** came from her home country of Mexico. The Mexican government declared her paintings national treasures. Today all her works can be viewed in Mexican art galleries and museums.

Vocabulary Study

A **Choose and write the correct word.**

> routinely   auctioned   appealing   severely   recognition

1. Mona Lisa's smile is so ___________ to many people.

2. William Zinsser achieved ___________ as a great writer.

3. Nowadays, many great paintings are being ___________ off.

4. Lots of people were ___________ injured in the explosion.

5 Some regulations are ___________ ignored by greedy companies.

B **Replace the underlined words with a synonym from the box.**

> directly   intense   glare   complicated   rigid

1. We were disappointed with their <u>inflexible</u> viewpoints.

2. Everybody was taken aback by her cold <u>stare</u>.

3. Many people were intimidated by the <u>intricate</u> structure of the system.

4. Britney looked <u>straight</u> to Emily's eyes.

5. The killers dealt the innocent villagers a <u>severe</u> blow.

Main idea

This story is about _______________.
   a. painting   b. a Latin America artist
   c. Latin America art   d. Frida Kahlo's husband

Paragraph Understanding

Choose the correct answer.

1. Paragraph ___   She learned to paint after a serious injury.
2. Paragraph ___   Since her death, she has become very famous in Mexico.
3. Paragraph ___   One of Frida Kahlo's works is the most expensive Latin American painting ever sold.
4. Paragraph ___   Frida was not widely recognized as a great artist in her lifetime.

Looking for detail

Circle the correct answer.

1. Frida Kahlo's most famous painting is ___________.
   a. bright   b. large
   c. small   d. complicated

2. When she was married to Diego Rivera, she ___________.
   a. continued to suffer   b. stopped painting
   c. received a lot of fame   d. injured herself badly

3. Which paragraph describes the accident Frida Kahlo suffered?
   a. Paragraph 1   b. Paragraph 2
   c. Paragraph   d. Paragraph 4

4. What can we conclude about Frida Kahlo's works today?
   a. Everybody in Mexico knows about them.
   b. Her husband's work is still more famous.
   c. They are shared with schools across Mexico.
   d. Nobody outside of Mexico knows about them.

Developing Skills

Rearrange the words below to make correct sentences.

1. are   art   museums   places   wonderful   to   visit

____

2. Kahlo   Frida   is   Mexican   a   artist   renowned

____

3. know   a   do   to   picture   you   how   paint

____

4. is   favorite   art   your   piece   of   what

____

5. is painting   my   called   definitely   favorite   the   Sunflowers

____

 T28   ## Summary & Listening Practice

Read the paragraph and fill in as many blanks as you can.
Then listen to the recording and fill in the rest of the blanks.

When one of Frida Kahlo's works was sold for more than one million dollars, it set a ① ___________ as the most expensive Latin American painting ever sold. This painting, perhaps Frida's most famous ever, is a self-portrait of the Mexican artist. It shows the ② ___________ of a woman who suffered awful ③ ___________ as a teenager. Although Frida was not widely recognized as a great ④ ___________ in her lifetime, since her death her paintings have become ⑤ ___________ treasures in Mexico.

15 Shedding "Light" on Moths

 T 29

1   Summer brings all kinds of insects. And some of them really bother us. For instance, there's a moth outside your window and it's trying to get inside your home. The reason it's trying to get inside is because it's attracted to the light inside. In more **extreme** cases, a moth will fly around a candle that is burning until it's so **dizzy** that it flies into the flame and burns up. Surprisingly, there's a **logical** reason why this happens.

2   Moths are actually very good at finding their way around. They often fly in a straight line, following the rays of the sun or the moon as a guide. They do not often bump or crash into things. When the moth is flying, it makes sure it is positioned so that the parallel rays of the sun or moon always hit its eyes at a certain angle. This ensures it keeps on a straight path during flight.

3   There is one problem with this **philosophy**, though. When another light appears nearby, it can confuse the moth. This is especially true when it flies near a street light, candlelight, or any other source of light. The moth will automatically change course when the light hits its eyes. The artificial light rays spread out in different directions mean they are not parallel like the sun or moon rays.

4   As a result, the moth will keep changing course in an effort to have the light fall on its eyes at the same angle. It becomes **disoriented**, tilting its body toward the light and then starting to fly in a circle. Soon, these circles grow smaller and smaller. In the end, the moth will fly directly into the light or sometimes, the candlelight, where it dies instantly. The interesting fact is that the moth was never attracted to the light in the first place. It was only distracted by the light.

Vocabulary Study

A Choose and write the correct word.

> dizzy   logical   extreme   philosophy   disoriented

1. Playing squash for too long makes me _____________.

2. The patient was too _____________ to be aware of his surroundings.

3. _____________ sports are very popular these days.

4. There must be an _____________ of the phenomena.

5. Their eco-friendly _____________ was appealing to consumers.

B Replace the underlined words with a synonym from the box.

> positioned   distracted   parallel   artificial   instantly

1. The first <u>man-made</u> satellite was produced by Russians.

2. The toys were neatly <u>arranged</u> in rows.

3. After receiving his letter, Julie replied to it <u>promptly</u>.

4. Before long, the public's attention was <u>diverted</u> from the issue.

5. The absence of <u>corresponding</u> structures is not easy to understand.

Main idea

This story is about _______________.

   a. light   b. flying

   c. moths   d. insects

Paragraph Understanding

Choose the correct answer.

1. Paragraph ___ Moths fly in a position that is parallel to the sun's rays or the moon's rays.

2. Paragraph ___ Sometimes moths seem like they want to break into your home.

3. Paragraph ___ In extreme cases, the moth will fly right into the light, even if it is a candlelight.

4. Paragraph ___ More than one source of light can confuse the moth.

Looking for detail

Circle the correct answer.

1. Moths often fly ___________.
   a. into objects
   b. in a straight line
   c. bumping into things
   d. away from light

2. What do moths follow as a guide?
   a. Sun and moon rays
   b. Candle lights
   c. Their sense of smell
   d. Artificial lights

3. Which paragraph describes the end result of a moth chasing two lights?
   a. Paragraph 1
   b. Paragraph 2
   c. Paragraph 3
   d. Paragraph 4

4. If there is a fire burning in a room with a moth, ___________.
   a. it will not fly in circles
   b. it will likely kill itself
   c. it will be scared and fly away
   d. it will certainly stop flying

Developing Skills

Rearrange the words below to make correct sentences.

1. candlelight a moth into night our flew last

____

2. I was down dizzy after practice that so I had to lie

____

3. ran his course this morning usual Ted

____

4. the heat this summer is the most extreme ever

____

5. it appears flame killed the moth itself by flying into a

____

T 30 Summary & Listening Practice

Read the paragraph and fill in as many blanks as you can.
Then listen to the recording and fill in the rest of the blanks.

Summer brings all kinds of insects, even moths. For instance, there might be a moth that looks like it wants to get ① ___________ your home. It's a ② ___________ that's leading it into your home. Moths fly in a position that is ③ ___________ to the rays of the sun or the moon. However, more than one ④ ___________ of light, like a lamp or candlelight, can confuse the moth. In extreme cases, the moth will fly right into the light and ⑤ ___________ itself.

16 The Dead Sea Scrolls Unraveled

T31

1 One of the most fascinating moments in recent history involves some old religious documents. In 1947, something very important was discovered near the Dead Sea, a body of water not far from Jerusalem — between Israel and Jordan. A shepherd who was searching for one of his goats found some scrolls wrapped in cloth and placed in jars in a cave. These scrolls — old pieces of paper — had an ancient form of writing on them that the shepherd couldn't read.

2 When **scholars** heard about the scrolls, they became very excited about the findings. Could these ancient writings be from the greatest book ever written? Realizing that the scrolls were from a long time ago, **archeologists** and scientists started exploring the area where the shepherd had found the first jars. More were soon found. Although some were very long, most were quite short, sometimes no bigger than a postage stamp.

3 Once these scrolls were all collected, scholars had to **translate** them. They quickly realized that they were mostly religious writings in Hebrew, Greek, and Aramaic — an ancient language no longer spoken. After much study, we now know that the scrolls were written centuries ago and then placed inside the caves. However, we don't know who the authors are or the exact dates they were written.

4 Some of the scholars and scientists examining the scrolls were hopeful that the documents would provide information about the Bible, one of the holiest books in the world today. They were **partially** correct. Among the scrolls are the oldest surviving copies of the Old Testament, the original **version** of the Christian Bible. Yet not every single scroll was religious. Scientists actually found one scroll that claimed to be a map of treasure buried in the area, but no one is sure whether it is real or not. In many ways, however, the Dead Sea Scrolls are an amazing historical treasure.

Vocabulary Study

A Choose and write the correct word.

> scholars   archeologists   translate   partially   versions

1. Surprisingly, the concert was ___________ successful.

2. The fact is that there are so many ___________ of the Bible.

3. All of the ___________ have degrees from the same university.

4. Robert can ___________ four languages.

5. In fact, ___________ can tell us who we really are.

B Replace the underlined words with a synonym from the box.

> fascinating   recognize   realize   holy   surviving

1. Some sea animals are difficult to <u>identify</u>.

2. Many researchers are complaining about the <u>existing</u> system.

3. The cozy restaurant was also famous for its <u>appealing</u> atmosphere.

4. The concept of relativity is not easy to <u>comprehend</u>.

5. This is a very <u>spiritual</u> text.

Main idea

This story is about _______________.

    a. recent inventions   b. important scrolls

    c. the Old Testament   d. old languages

Paragraph Understanding

Choose the correct answer.

1. Paragraph ___ Scholars soon found many other scrolls, but most were very small.

2. Paragraph ___ Once the scrolls were found, they had to be translated.

3. Paragraph ___ Among the Dead Sea Scrolls are the oldest surviving copies of the Old Testament.

4. Paragraph ___ The Dead Sea Scrolls were discovered by a shepherd in 1947.

Looking for detail

Circle the correct answer.

1. Which languages were the Dead Sea Scrolls not written in?
   a. Greek
   b. Aramaic
   c. Hebrew
   d. Latin

2. Who found the Dead Sea Scrolls?
   a. A scientist
   b. An archeologist
   c. A shepherd
   d. A linguist

3. Which paragraph talks about the translation of the Dead Sea Scrolls?
   a. Paragraph 1
   b. Paragraph 2
   c. Paragraph 3
   d. Paragraph 4

4. According to the passage, ___________.
   a. no one has found the treasure described in the Dead Sea Scrolls
   b. Hebrew teachers have translated all of the Dead Sea Scrolls
   c. the Dead Sea Scrolls led to new information about the New Testament
   d. nobody can understand exactly what the Dead Sea Scrolls say

Developing Skills

Rearrange the words below to make correct sentences.

1. translated   documents   were   the   by   the   woman

   ____

2. it   scholars   been   studying   have

   ____

3. some   texts   were   Sea   found   near   the   holy   Dead

   ____

4. speaks   in   the   world   Aramaic   nobody   anymore

   ____

5. my   cleaned   jars   the   that   we   used   mother

   ____

T 32   ## Summary & Listening Practice

Read the paragraph and fill in as many blanks as you can.
Then listen to the recording and fill in the rest of the blanks.

In 1947, a shepherd happened to find the Dead Sea Scrolls when looking for a lost goat ① _____________ the Dead Sea. Soon, ② _____________ found many other scrolls that held much importance, but most were very small documents. After the scrolls were found, they had to be ③ _____________ from several languages. Interestingly, one of the ④ _____________ parts of the Dead Sea Scrolls is that they hold the oldest ⑤ _____________ copies of the Old Testament.

17 The Deepest Part of the World

 T 33

1 Mt. Everest is famous for being the highest point on Earth. But what gets much less attention is the deepest part of the ocean, a dark and strange place located in the Pacific Ocean. Did you know that this place is actually deeper than Mt. Everest is high? Well, it's true.

2 It was only in 1951 that scientists learned this remarkable fact. A research ship was mapping the ocean floor near the Mariana Islands using echo sounders, instruments that bounce signals off the ocean floor. Most of the area around the islands is two or three miles deep — something the scientists were well **aware** of. But one day, the echo sounders suddenly showed an amazing depth of seven miles! They named the watery canyon, which was six miles deeper than the Grand Canyon, the Mariana Trench.

3 Actually, the Mariana Trench is a long chain of **trenches** in the middle of the Pacific Ocean, and also the deepest one ever measured. The trenches are all **extremely** dark and narrow. Because the water is so cold and the pressure is more than eight tons per square inch — enough to crush most submarines — researchers believed that nothing could survive that far down.

4 For nine years, the mystery of possible sea life in the Mariana Trench remained **unsolved**. In 1960, two scientists went straight down into the Mariana Trench in a specially built underwater vessel that was designed to withstand the **tremendous** pressures. When they reached the bottom of the ocean floor, seven miles down, they turned on a searchlight and looked out through one of the vessel's portholes. What they saw amazed them. A fish peacefully swam by, hardly noticing the two men and their vessel. Although the trip took more than nine hours, it proved that life does exist in the great depths of the Mariana Trench.

Vocabulary Study

A Choose and write the correct word.

> aware   trenches   extremely   unsolved   tremendous

1. World War I was mostly fought in ___________.

2. When choosing a career, be ___________ cautious.

3. Unfortunately, the case remained ___________.

4. We're keenly ___________ of the situation in Iraq.

5. Lisa has made ___________ efforts to realize her dream.

B Replace the underlined words with a synonym from the box.

> attention   peak   remarkable   measure   withstand

1. The <u>summit</u> of this mountain is just above us.

2. Success often depends on one's ability to <u>endure</u> hardship.

3. We're doing everything to raise <u>awareness</u> about the disease.

4. It might be impossible to completely <u>assess</u> one's ability.

5. Naomi is <u>noteworthy</u> for her exceptional achievement.

Main idea

This story is about ___________.

   a. the depths of an ocean   b. the most interesting ocean

   c. Scotland   d. mountains and oceans

Paragraph Understanding

Choose the correct answer.

1. Paragraph ___   Researchers used to think nothing lived at the bottom of the Mariana Trench.

2. Paragraph ___   In 1960, life was found at the bottom of the Mariana Trench.

3. Paragraph ___   Most people don't know that the deepest part of the ocean is higher than the highest mountain.

4. Paragraph ___   In 1951, scientists discovered that the Mariana Trench is seven miles deep.

Looking for detail

Circle the correct answer.

1. Mapping the ocean floor is done by using __________.
   a. echo sounders
   b. a measuring stick
   c. scuba divers
   d. submarines

2. Researchers were surprised by the Mariana Trench because __________.
   a. there's so much life there
   b. it's so dark
   c. it's so shallow
   d. it's so deep

3. Which paragraph describes the life found at the bottom of the Mariana Trench?
   a. Paragraph 1
   b. Paragraph 2
   c. Paragraph 3
   d. Paragraph 4

4. It's very likely that we __________.
   a. will never reach the bottom of the Mariana Trench
   b. need to determine how deep the Mariana Trench is
   c. have a lot to learn about the Mariana Trench
   d. will never know if there is life at the bottom of the ocean floor

Developing Skills

Rearrange the words below to make correct sentences.

1. my his brother me with hug crushed

____

2. can bounce ships signals the ocean off floor

____

3. Mariana the part of the Pacific deepest Ocean is the Trench

____

4. war for ended the peacefully him

____

5. remarkable the made a scientist discovery

____

T34   Summary & Listening Practice

Read the paragraph and fill in as many blanks as you can.
Then listen to the recording and fill in the rest of the blanks.

Although Mt. Everest is the highest peak on Earth, the Mariana Trench is actually the ① ___________ point on Earth we know. Scientists ② ___________ that the Mariana Trench is seven miles deep, six miles deeper than the Grand Canyon, in 1951. At first, ③ ___________ thought that there could be nothing living at the bottom of the ④ ___________. But they were wrong. In 1960, scientists found that there were fish in the ⑤ ___________ of the Mariana Trench.

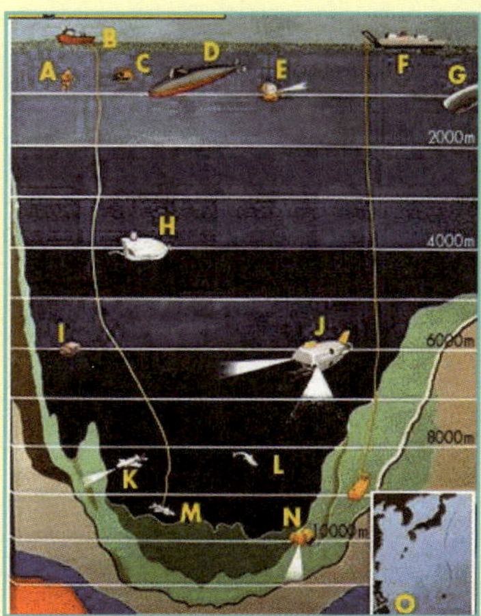

Krakatoa

 T35

1 Did you know the history of the world's greatest natural explosion? In the 17th century, an island was formed in the Indian Ocean when a volcano called Krakatoa erupted. For 200 years, the Indonesian volcano had been **dormant**. But in 1883, all that changed. For three months explosions rocked the island where the Krakatoa volcano was. Then, on August 27, an incredible **blast** exploded. The eruption was so loud that it was heard up to 5,000 kilometers away! When the explosions finally stopped, the volcano was completely gone from the surface of the Earth.

2 However, the **aftermath** of Krakatoa's eruption would live on for some time. At the time of the explosion, rocks were thrown more than 20 kilometers into the air, and the ash **darkened** the sky. People living up to 150 kilometers away were forced to light lamps at noon to see. Later, the dust was carried around the world three times by the upper atmosphere's air currents. Sunrises and sunsets turned red for two years. During that time, world temperatures dropped several degrees because some of the sun's heat was blocked out by the dust.

3 Unfortunately, things got worse. The most serious consequence of the volcanic activity was the huge waves that rolled out around the area. On the water, boats were overturned by tidal waves. Yet it was on land that the most serious effects were felt. When the waves reached nearby shores, entire villages were **wiped** out, similar to the tsunami of 2004. In the end, approximately 36,000 people were killed by the 1883 Krakatoa explosion.

4 Some scientists think that Krakatoa might have a comeback. Over the past 60 years or so, small explosions in the area have caused land to form where Krakatoa used to be. No one knows what will happen to those who live nearby if the "Child of Krakatoa" erupts again.

Vocabulary Study

A Choose and write the correct word.

> dormant   blast   aftermath   darken   wiped

1. The ____________ of the tsunami was overwhelming.

2. Admiral Lee ____________ out many Japanese invaders.

3. The incident might ____________ their future.

4. Actually, the club remained ____________ for many years.

5. A nuclear ____________ might kill thousands of people instantly.

B Replace the underlined words with a synonym from the box.

> formed   changed   forced   blocked   overturned

1. Its progress was <u>hindered</u> by the communists.

2. They <u>transformed</u> the building into a hospital.

3. When their boat <u>capsized</u>, there was no one to help them.

4. The structure <u>materialized</u> as a huge tomb.

5. Many people were <u>coerced</u> into working for hours.

Main idea

This story is about ________________.

    a. famous volcanoes   b. a 20th century explosion

    c. weather patterns   d. a volcanic eruption

Paragraph Understanding

Choose the correct answer.

1. Paragraph ___   Krakatoa erupted violently in 1883.
2. Paragraph ___   Its effects could be felt up to two years later.
3. Paragraph ___   Krakatoa might emerge again.
4. Paragraph ___   In total, tens of thousands of people died.

Looking for detail

Circle the correct answer.

1. Before Krakatoa erupted in 1883, there were explosions for
   __________.

   a. one day   b. three months
   c. three days   d. one month

2. Why was the world's weather affected by Krakatoa's eruption?
   a. The sun disappeared.
   b. There were too many tsunamis.
   c. There were no sunsets or sunrises.
   d. Dust was caught in air currents.

3. Which paragraph talks about the location of Krakatoa?
   a. Paragraph 1   b. Paragraph 2
   c. Paragraph 3   d. Paragraph 4

4. In the future, __________.
   a. Krakatoa will erupt again
   b. the Indian Ocean will vanish
   c. there won't be anymore tsunamis
   d. Krakatoa might explode again

Developing Skills

Rearrange the words below to make correct sentences.

1. the   about   Earth   billion   formed   four   and   a   years   half   ago

   ____

2. I   if   tsunami   there   will   be   sometimes   another   wonder

   ____

3. consequence   was   one   of   my   that   actions

   ____

4. are   volcanoes   time   there   erupting   all   the

   ____

5. 100°C   learned   at   water   we   boils   that

   ____

🔊 T36   Summary & Listening Practice

Read the paragraph and fill in as many blanks as you can.
Then listen to the recording and fill in the rest of the blanks.

Krakatoa ① ____________ violently in 1883, after 200 years of being dormant in the Indian Ocean. Its ② ____________ could be felt up to two years later, with red sunrises and red sunsets. In total, tens of thousands of people ③ ____________. Tsunamis killed many people in boats at the time and many people on ④ ____________. Krakatoa might erupt again in the near ⑤ ____________.

1. Communication is essential to our survival. But for those who are deaf, the world can be **vastly** different. Most people are aware that the deaf communicate in sign language. However, in many cases, the deaf cannot easily communicate because of the many different forms of sign language around the world. In truth, there are about 50 sign languages "spoken" in various countries.

2. In the United States, deaf people use what is referred to as American Sign Language, or ASL. ASL, on the other hand, is a true language all on its own. In ASL, gestures represent whole words, so it is not **technically** signed English. Others in the deaf community around the world consider ASL as **clumsy** and artificial and do not use it often.

3. You might be asking yourself, what exactly is a true language? Well, it's made up of small symbols — that have no meaning on their own — but can be combined into meaningful units of "speech." This is not very different from how the English alphabet is constructed. Individual letters all have their own sounds, and when put together, form words that have **distinct** meanings. Second, a real language has proper grammar rules used to put words together. Third, a true language will change and adapt over time.

4. ASL has all of these characteristics. The language draws on not only the communicator's hands, but also their face and body. For example, the shape of the hands creates one element of a sign. This is done by moving the hands in relation to the body and creating another sign. Yet one cannot ignore the expression on someone's face. The mere act of tilting the head forward and raising the eyebrows while signing makes any question a statement. Finally, like languages everywhere, ASL is constantly **evolving** and adapting to new influences.

Vocabulary Study

A Choose and write the correct word.

> vastly   clumsy   technically   distinct   evolved

1. Their views were ___________ different from ours.

2. The tomato is ___________ classified as a fruit.

3. I'm always ___________ when handling knives.

4. The newspaper is well known for its ___________ views on many issues.

5. Some scientists claim that birds ___________ from reptiles.

B Replace the underlined words with a synonym from the box.

> essential   various   combined   constructed   ignore

1. Eventually, the two companies were <u>merged</u>.

2. The watch was carefully <u>assembled</u> by a skilled worker.

3. The writing system has played a <u>crucial</u> role in imparting knowledge.

4. It is rude to <u>disregard</u> the opinions of your parents.

5. Surprisingly, Korean society is made up of <u>diverse</u> ethnic groups.

Main idea

This story is about _______________.

   a. written languages   b. deaf people

   c. a non-verbal language   d. how languages are taught

Paragraph Understanding

Choose the correct answer.

1. Paragraph ___   A true language has individual letters and grammar rules.
2. Paragraph ___   There are more than 50 deaf languages.
3. Paragraph ___   ASL is evolving constantly.
4. Paragraph ___   American Sign Language is a language all on its own.

Looking for detail

Circle the correct answer.

1. The deaf communicate in __________ language.
   a. dead
   c. mark
   b. old
   d. sign

2. True languages are made of __________.
   a. small symbols
   c. speakers and listeners
   b. voiced thoughts
   d. large symbols

3. Which paragraph talks about how many sign languages there are?
   a. Paragraph 1
   c. Paragraph 3
   b. Paragraph 2
   d. Paragraph 4

4. In 100 years, ASL could __________.
   a. be very different than it is today
   b. will be the same as it is today
   c. will be used by everyone in the world
   d. will have disappeared

Developing Skills

Rearrange the words below to make correct sentences.

1. I'm   play   really   when   I   the   piano   clumsy

   ____

2. understand   we   try   and   deaf   should   people

   ____

3. did   you   sign   when   language   learn

   ____

4. plot   one   of   the   story   element   I   liked   was   the

   ____

5. it   a   mere   five   to   receive   an   minutes   answer   took

   ____

T38   Summary & Listening Practice

Read the paragraph and fill in as many blanks as you can.
Then listen to the recording and fill in the rest of the blanks.

Many people are unaware that deaf people can
① ___________. In fact, deaf people may not be able
to speak, but they have 50 different sign languages.
American Sign Language, for instance, is a language
all on its own. It is a true ② ___________ because it
has individual letters and grammar rules. Also, ASL
is evolving ③ ___________. While it evolves and
adapts, deaf people continue to use the
④ ___________ and head ⑤ ___________ to indicate
their meaning.

PRIMITIVE PEOPLE

Pre-reading activity

1. What did Neanderthals look like?
2. What happened 35,000 years ago?
3. How were Cro-Magnons different from Neanderthals?

 T 39

1. Have you ever wondered what our ancestors looked like thousands of years ago? Well, for centuries, bones from the Stone Age have been found in locations all over Europe and western Asia. Some of these skeletons even resemble the bones of today's humans. But one group of bones remains more unique than any others — that of Neanderthals. The Neanderthals had **specific** characteristics which include: a very small chin, a **bulging** ridge above the eyes, and arm and leg bones that were extremely strong and heavy. This meant they had very large muscles. Neanderthals were much stronger than modern humans.

2. However, they were more than just cavemen with muscles. Neanderthals had other characteristics that are similar to ours today. They were intelligent, for instance and could survive in difficult environments. They knew how to make excellent stone tools, were good hunters, and, because of their strength, could kill large animals with their bare hands. Living in small groups, early Neanderthals may have spoken a language that either disappeared or merged with another **dialect**. Furthermore, they buried the dead, something unique to the human race.

3. Yet 35,000 years ago, the Neanderthals **vanished**. No one knows why they disappeared, however. To this day, many questions remain about their disappearance. Were they all killed? Did they die out from changes in the environment? Or did they evolve into modern humans?

4. There was a time when scientists thought that Neanderthals were our ancestors, but now they believe they were more like our cousins than our grandparents. The Cro-Magnons, who lived at the same time as the Neanderthals, are human beings' true ancestors. However, questions remain about them, too. Although the Cro-Magnons were smaller and weaker, archaeologists do know that they were more intelligent and **inventive**. That was why they survived and left many things to modern humans.

Vocabulary Study

A Choose and write the correct word.

> specific   bulging   dialect   vanished   inventive

1. With her eyes __________, Erica stared at me.

2. The __________ writer thought of an amazing story.

3. These products are aimed at __________ groups of women.

4. Sadly, many rare species __________ from the earth.

5. In fact, there are many regional __________ in America.

B Replace the underlined words with a synonym from the box.

> characteristic   lifted   intelligent   ancestors   modern

1. The <u>predecessors</u> of the modern computer were huge.

2. Eric is very <u>knowledgeable</u> about English grammar.

3. Current films are quite <u>different</u> from earlier ones.

4. Generosity is one of the <u>attributes</u> of great people.

5. Several people <u>elevated</u> the rocks from the ground.

Main idea

This story is about __________.

    a. Neanderthals   b. humankind's ancestors

    c. human beings   d. a history of the world

Paragraph Understanding

Choose the correct answer.

1. Paragraph ____   However, tens of thousands of years ago, Neanderthals disappeared.
2. Paragraph ____   They also had other traits similar to human beings, like intelligence and language.
3. Paragraph ____   Neanderthal bones resemble human bones.
4. Paragraph ____   Today we know that our true ancestors were the Cro-Magnons.

Looking for detail

Circle the correct answer.

1. Why did Neanderthals vanish thousands of years ago?
   a. There was a natural disaster.
   b. They died with the dinosaurs.
   c. Cro-Magnons killed them all.
   d. Nobody knows.

2. Compared to Neanderthals, Cro-Magnons were not ____________.
   a. more intelligent
   b. more inventive
   c. smaller
   d. stronger

3. Which paragraph describes what Neanderthals did with their dead?
   a. Paragraph 1
   b. Paragraph 2
   c. Paragraph 3
   d. Paragraph 4

4. Cro-Magnons probably survived because of ____________.
   a. their strength
   b. the weather
   c. their intelligence
   d. their size

Developing Skills

Rearrange the words below to make correct sentences.

1. many beings have distinct human characteristics

   ____

2. in buried the bones a graveyard We

   ____

3. Heather mountains when she was vanished in the

   ____

4. people could very be inventive primitive

   ____

5. mother I my very resemble much

   ____

T 40   Summary & Listening Practice

Read the paragraph and fill in as many blanks as you can.
Then listen to the recording and fill in the rest of the blanks.

Neanderthal bones ① ___________ human bones. But Neanderthals shared more than just similar bone structure with modern humans. They also had similar ② ___________, like the ③ ___________ to use tools, the need to bury the dead and, perhaps, the ability to speak a language. Yet 35,000 years ago, they suddenly vanished, and no one is sure why. Today, however, we know that our true ④ ___________ were the Cro-Magnons, who survived because they were more intelligent and more ⑤ ___________ than the Neanderthals.

Developing Advanced Reading Skills

BuildUp Reading

Workbook

Level 2

WorldCom ELT

01 THE CHANGING WORLD

Vocabulary & Idioms

origin
n. beginning, the first stage of existence
Ex. *The origin of this type of music dates way back to several centuries ago.*

gigantic
adj. very large, enormous
Ex. *The moon looks gigantic tonight.*

continent
n. one of the main landmasses of the globe
Ex. *There are seven continents in the world.*

approximately
adv. nearly, roughly
Ex. *There are approximately fifty jellybeans in the jar.*

drift
v. to proceed or move unhurriedly and smoothly
Ex. *The snow slowly drifted down the slopes.*

massive
adj. large, having great mass
Ex. *The bomb created a massive explosion.*

trench
n. a long, narrow ditch
Ex. *We hid in trenches during the raid.*

intense
adj. acute, strong, existing in a high or extreme degree
Ex. *An intense light showed in her eyes.*

molten
adj. melted, liquefied by heat
Ex. *The volcano is full of molten rock.*

surface
n. the outer face, outside, or exterior boundary of something
Ex. *The diver swam back up to the surface of the water.*

contrary
adj. opposite
Ex. *Contrary to what you think, I did not eat your last piece of bread.*

process
n. a systematic series of actions directed to some end
Ex. *The process of photosynthesis is very complicated.*

A Choose the best word(s) to fill in the blank.

1. Let's dig a few ____________ in our yard.

   a. continents   b. origins   c. trenches   d. processes

2. The heat is too ____________ to be outside.

   a. massive   b. intense   c. molten   d. contrary

3. What a[n] ____________ house!

   a. gigantic   b. intense   c. molten   d. sad

4. Seattle is ____________ 20 miles away.

   a. approximately   b. eventually   c. appropriately   d. politely

5. The whole laundry ____________ takes about an hour.

   a. trench   b. continent   c. origin   d. process

B Choose the correct form of the word to fill in the blanks.

1. Let's follow the river to its ____________.

   a. originate   b. originally   c. origin

2. On the ____________, oil is much lighter than water.

   a. contrast   b. contrary   c. contrarily

3. The ____________ desert ran for miles.

   a. mass   b. massive   c. massively

4. Have you ever traveled to another ____________?

   a. continental   b. continentally   c. continent

5. The message ____________ on the board is difficult to understand.

   a. written   b. writer   c. writing

Listening  T41

Listen to the dialog and choose the best answer.

1. What is the lecture mainly about?
   a. The formation of Europe
   b. African tribes
   c. Ocean ecology
   d. More history of the world's origins

2. What two land masses did Gondwana break up into during the late Jurassic?
   a. Asia and East Gondwana
   b. Laurasia and the Canadian Shield
   c. Africa and East Gondwana
   d. Australia and Antarctica

3. How many landmasses were added to Gondwana in the formation of Pangaea?
   a. One
   b. Two
   c. Three
   d. Four

Grammar Review

Choose the correct one.

1. There are ____________ that we need to overcome.
   [too much obstacles / so many obstacles / too many obstacle]

2. Tom was ____________ a national hero.
   [referred as / referred / referred to as]

3. ____________ accident, Sam couldn't participate in the event.
   [Since / Because of the / Because the]

4. Information technology ____________ the world we live in.
   [is constantly changing / are constant change / is constantly changed]

5. Marie loves romantic comedies, ____________ likes horror movies.
   [despite her husband / because her husband / while her husband]

THE TROJAN WAR

Vocabulary & Idioms

renowned *adj.* having widespread fame
Ex. *The singer is renowned for her unique style and grace.*

penetrate *v.* to pierce, to pass through, to enter the interior of
Ex. *When the dog bit you, did it penetrate the skin?*

creative *adj.* having originality, clever
Ex. *What a creative painting!*

give up to surrender, to abandon hope
Ex. *I gave up on the idea of winning a million dollars in the lottery.*

capture *v.* to take by force
Ex. *The captured rabbits looked very frightened.*

trick *n.* a crafty device intended to deceive or cheat
Ex. *I know several magic tricks.*

tale *n.* a narrative that tells of some real or imaginary event
Ex. *Have you ever heard the tale of Honest Abe?*

remains *n.* all that is left of other parts that have been taken away
Ex. *These statues are the only remains of the building.*

strait *n.* a narrow passage of water connecting two large bodies of water
Ex. *Korea and Japan are separated by a strait.*

toll *n.* a fee exacted by the government or local authorities for a right or privilege
Ex. *How much is the toll for using this road?*

moor *v.* to secure a ship to a particular place
Ex. *Sailors moor their ships at the dock.*

thus *adv.* accordingly, in this manner
Ex. *He was thus taken to prison for his unjust behavior.*

Vocabulary Review

A Choose the best word(s) to fill in the blank.

1. The actor is ______________ throughout the world.
   a. creative   b. renowned   c. molten   d. ingenious

2. We will continue fighting and we won't ______________.
   a. penetrate   b. give up   c. show up   d. drown

3. He ate the ______________ of the pizza.
   a. strait   b. tale   c. remains   d. toll

4. We had to pay a ______________ to cross the bridge.
   a. tale   b. strait   c. check   d. toll

5. ______________, he was able to win the match due to his many hours of practice.
   a. Thus   b. Entirely   c. Truly   d. Unjustly

B Choose the correct form of the word to fill in the blanks.

1. At last, the police ______________ the thief.
   a. captive   b. captured   c. captivity

2. There are several ways of ______________ at this situation.
   a. look   b. looking   c. looked

3. The story was very ______________.
   a. creative   b. creation   c. create

4. Their rude behavior ______________ many people.
   a. angered   b. angry   c. angrily

5. They ______________ that she was insane.
   a. conclusive   b. conclusion   c. concluded

Listen to the dialog and choose the best answer.

1. What is the lecture mainly about?
   a. The *Illiad*
   b. Greek history
   c. The Trojan War
   d. Famous scholars

2. What is true about the Illiad?
   a. It was written by Bart.
   b. Scholars know the exact date in which it was written.
   c. It is one of the oldest pieces of Greek literature.
   d. It is written in the form of a novel.

3. Homer was a ______________.
   a. blind poet
   b. deaf musician
   c. criminal
   d. philosopher

Grammar Review

Choose the correct one.

1. William Zinsser is one of ______________ in America.
   [the greater writer/ greatest writer/ the greatest writers]

2. World War I ______________ 1914.
   [broke out in/ has broken out in/ broke out on]

3. I came across a strange man ______________.
   [call Henry/ called Henry/ calling Henry]

4. ______________, Jenny came across an old friend.
   [Walking along the street/ Walked along the street/ Walk along the streets]

5. If I were a bird, I ______________ to you.
   [will fly/ could fly/ can fly]

Vocabulary & Idioms

cuddly   *adj.*   inviting hugs, huggable
       Ex.   *The child was holding a cuddly teddy bear.*

muscle   *n.*   a tissue that allows the body to move
       Ex.   *If you exercise, your muscles will grow stronger.*

strengthen   *v.*   to make stronger, to give strength to
       Ex.   *The marathon runner is strengthening his legs.*

balance   *n.*   the ability to maintain bodily equilibrium
       Ex.   *My balance is very poor.*

domestic   *adj.*   related to the home
       Ex.   *She is a domestic housewife.*

youngster   *n.*   a child, a young person
       Ex.   *The youngsters are learning how to read.*

meadow   *n.*   a tract of grassland
       Ex.   *The meadow is full of rabbits during this time of year.*

obvious   *adj.*   easily seen, recognized or understood
       Ex.   *The answer is obvious.*

predator   *n.*   an organism that lives by eating other organisms
       Ex.   *The tiger is a ferocious predator.*

extend   *v.*   to reach or spread out to
       Ex.   *I extended my hand out to her.*

make-believe   *adj.*   playful pretense
       Ex.   *The little girl had a make-believe tea party in the backyard.*

social skill   the skill of making friends and getting along with others
       Ex.   *It is important to have good social skills.*

A Choose the best word(s) to fill in the blank.

1. My rabbit is so soft and ____________.
   a. domestic   b. cuddly   c. obvious   d. make-believe

2. The ____________ sat watching TV and playing with his toys.
   a. youngster   b. predator   c. rooster   d. chef

3. It's pretty ____________ that a storm is approaching
   a. domestic   b. cuddly   c. obvious   d. make-believe

4. My ____________ are aching from yesterday's workout.
   a. muscles   b. youngsters   c. roosters   d. chefs

5. Beware of ____________ that live in the woods.
   a. youngsters   b. roosters   c. trees   d. predators

B Choose the correct form of the word to fill in the blanks.

1. I am ____________ my muscles.
   a. strength   b. strengthening   c. strengthened

2. I stood ____________ at the wonderful sight.
   a. stare   b. staring   c. stared

3. How far does the river ____________?
   a. extend   b. extent   c. extension

4. The ballerina's ____________ is impeccable.
   a. balance   b. balanced   c. balances

5. The ____________ of the species is in danger.
   a. survive   b. survival   c. survivors

Listening  T43

Listen to the dialog and choose the best answer.

1. What is the lecture mainly about?
   a. Young animals learning as they play
   b. Predators and their hunting skills
   c. Baby monkeys making friends
   d. Different types of meadows

2. What is true about young animals?
   a. They are not afraid of predators.
   b. They are born with most of the skills they need.
   c. They learn many survival skills at an early age.
   d. They learn very slowly.

3. Predators practice _____________ at an early age.
   a. speaking   b. hunting   c. joking   d. sleeping

Grammar Review

Choose the correct one.

1. In fact, nothing is _____________ health.
   [more important then / more important than / most important then]

2. Do you know _____________?
   [where Chris lives / how does Chris live / where did Chris live]

3. The medicine will definitely _____________ the pain.
   [helped ease / helping to ease / help ease]

4. Surprisingly, we saw a stranger _____________ our house.
   [broken into / break into / to break out of]

5. They _____________ the bus station by then.
   [may have left / may had left / might had leaving]

Vocabulary & Idioms

construction   *n.*   the building or making of something, usually a house or building
Ex.   *The workers are working on the construction of a new highway.*

lawn   *n.*   a plot of grass that is part of a residence
Ex.   *My father is mowing the lawn.*

laundry   *n.*   clothes that have been or are to be washed
Ex.   *I have a lot of dirty laundry this week.*

decade   *n.*   ten years
Ex.   *How many decades has it been since World War II?*

set fire   to start a fire
Ex.   *Lightning set fire to the forest.*

violent   *adj.*   acting with uncontrolled rough force
Ex.   *The violent wind blew and blew.*

democracy   *n.*   government by the people
Ex.   *The American government is an example of democracy.*

blast   *v.*   to shoot
Ex.   *The police blasted the criminal.*

cannon   *n.*   a mounted gun for firing heavy projectiles
Ex.   *The cannon blasted away.*

elevator   *n.*   a moving platform that carries passengers or freight from one level to another
Ex.   *A limited number of people can ride in the elevator.*

despite   *prep.*   in spite of; notwithstanding
Ex.   *Despite the storm, the children still played outside.*

occupy   *v.*   to be a resident or tenant of, to live in
Ex.   *This apartment is occupied.*

Vocabulary Review

A Choose the best word(s) to fill in the blank.

1. Have you finished washing the ______________ yet?
   a. laundry   b. lawn   c. construction   d. elevator

2. ______________ the doctor's efforts, the disease could not be cured.
   a. Because of   b. Due to   c. During   d. Despite

3. The ______________ in front of our house is quite large.
   a. laundry   b. lawn   c. construction   d. elevator

4. I haven't seen one of those in ______________ .
   a. decades   b. laundry   c. lawns   d. lights

5. The ______________ storm knocked over a few trees and power lines.
   a. make-believe   b. violent   c. quiet   d. normal

B Choose the correct form of the word to fill in the blanks.

1. This house was once ______________ by a famous celebrity.
   a. occupation   b. occupied   c. occupant

2. We must ride the ______________ to get to the top floor.
   a. elevation   b. elevator   c. elevating

3. ______________ of a new building is taking place across the street.
   a. Constructive   b. Construct   c. Construction

4. The earthquake was one of the major ______________ last year.
   a. disastrous   b. disastrously   c. disasters

5. The children ______________ set fire to their house.
   a. accident   b. accidentally   c. accidental

Listen to the dialog and choose the best answer.

1. What is the lecture mainly about?
   a. Animals at the White House
   b. The children of Presidents
   c. The White House's elevator
   d. Unusual facts about the White House

2. Which of the following did NOT happen in the White House?
   a. Tad Lincoln blasted a door.　　　b. Sheep roamed the lawns.
   c. Tigers guarded the front gate.　　d. A pony rode in the elevator.

3. How many years has the White House housed Presidents?
   a. 20　　　　　b. 180　　　　　c. 100　　　　　d. 207

Grammar Review

Choose the correct one.

1. We signed the contract with them, _____________ some disagreements.
   [although there was/ though were there/though there were]

2. _____________ to be cared about.
   [Every student deserves/ Each students deserve/ Every students deserve]

3. While _____________, Alex made many friends.
   [lived here/ live there/ living there]

4. The writer _____________ books since 2006.
   [have published few/ has published many/ published much]

5. That was a truly _____________.
   [amazing story/ amazed stories/ amazing stories]

Vocabulary & Idioms

lead   *n.*   a heavy, slightly soft, bluish gray metal
Ex. Is it made out of lead?

millennium   *n.*   one thousand years
Ex. We have just entered into the second millennium.

entrepreneur   *n.*   a person who organizes and manages an enterprise
Ex. Who is the entrepreneur who started this business?

practice   *v.*   to do as a job or profession
Ex. He practices law.

religion   *n.*   a set of beliefs concerning the nature of the universe
Ex. My religion is Buddhism.

composed of   made of
Ex. Ice cream is mostly composed of milk.

transform   *v.*   to change in form, material, or structure
Ex. The caterpillar transforms into a beautiful butterfly.

transfer   *v.*   to move from one place, person, or thing to another
Ex. I need to transfer funds to my bank account.

key   *n.*   a means of access, control, or possession
Ex. I know the key to getting better at English.

prolong   *v.*   to lengthen out in time, cause to continue longer
Ex. The flight was prolonged a few hours due to bad weather.

code   *n.*   a system of communicating in secrecy
Ex. The letter was written in code.

mislead   *v.*   to trick or deceive
Ex. I was misled into believing that the story was real.

A Choose the best word(s) to fill in the blank.

1. What job does he ____________ ?
   a. transfer   b. practice   c. prolong   d. mislead

2. We must find a way to read this message written in ____________ .
   a. religion   b. a millennium   c. code   d. shapes

3. I know the ____________ to getting there faster.
   a. religion   b. code   c. key   d. day

4. I wish I could ____________ my vacation a few days.
   a. practice   b. prolong   c. transfer   d. transform

5. The ____________ runs several thriving shops in town.
   a. entrepreneur   b. lizard   c. mongoose   d. temple

B Choose the correct form of the word to fill in the blanks.

1. Because of his illness, he's ____________ into a very thin skeleton of a person.
   a. transformative   b. transformed   c. transformation

2. Your explanation is very ____________ .
   a. misled   b. mislead   c. misleading

3. Every day I wake up ____________ of you.
   a. thinking   b. thinker   c. thought

4. We could ____________ them how to play basketball.
   a. teach   b. teacher   c. teachable

5. All we ____________ is a little more time.
   a. necessity   b. necessary   c. need

Listening  T45

Listen to the dialog and choose the best answer.

1. What is the lecture mainly about?
   a. How alchemists fooled people
   b. How to create gold from lead
   c. Modern chemistry
   d. Alchemists creating silver

2. What is true about the work of alchemists?
   a. It helped modern chemistry.
   b. It changed lead into gold.
   c. It is the key to modern science.
   d. People still practice alchemy.

3. Which of the following was NOT mentioned in the lecture?
   a. How alchemists fooled people
   b. Modern chemistry
   c. Alchemy as a major contribution
   d. The life of an alchemist

Grammar Review

Choose the correct one.

1. If I had been there with him, I ______________ his life.
   [could have saving/ could have saved/ can saved]

2. I have ______________ tell you.
   [important something/ important something to/ something important to]

3. The main reason was ______________ disliked him.
   [because of their/ that they/ because them]

4. You can be reassured that there are many ways to ______________.
   [kept your money safely/ keeping your money safe/ keep your money safe]

5. We were simply ______________ the sight.
   [amazed by/ amazing by/ amazing at]

Vocabulary & Idioms

daily   *adj.*   occurring every day, occurring frequently
       Ex.   *Playing the piano is one of my favorite daily activities.*

ordinary   *adj.*   normal, not special
       Ex.   *Today was not an ordinary day.*

marvelous   *adj.*   wonderful, amazing, excellent
       Ex.   *The food was just marvelous.*

invention   *n.*   a creation of something new
       Ex.   *The invention of the light bulb was a very important contribution to society.*

deaf   *adj.*   unable to hear
       Ex.   *The child was born deaf.*

desperately   *adv.*   with urgent need or desire
       Ex.   *I desperately need food right now.*

conduct   *v.*   to manage, to carry on
       Ex.   *The doctor conducted several tests to determine his illness.*

telegraph   *n.*   a communication system that sends and receives messages through electronic pulses
       Ex.   *Before the telephone was invented, most people used the telegraph.*

assistant   *n.*   a person who gives aid or support, a helper
       Ex.   *The scientist had several assistants in his laboratory.*

metal detector   an electronic device that can sense and find metal objects
       Ex.   *My neighbor was searching his yard with a metal detector.*

bullet   *n.*   a small metal projectile for firing from guns or small arms
       Ex.   *The policeman reloaded his gun with more bullets.*

motor   *n.*   a comparatively small and powerful engine
       Ex.   *The boat runs by motor.*

Vocabulary Review

A Choose the best word(s) to fill in the blank.

1. Brushing your teeth is a ____________ process for almost everyone.
   a. daily   b. lovely   c. truly   d. bleakly

2. The Empire State Building is a wonderful and ____________ structure.
   a. daily   b. ordinary   c. marvelous   d. deaf

3. I need an ____________ to help me do the job.
   a. assistant   b. alchemist   c. optimist   d. energizer

4. Is the gun out of ____________?
   a. juice   b. bullets   c. leaves   d. telegraphs

5. His ____________ began to beep as he came close to the pile of scrap metal.
   a. telegraph   b. metal detector   c. assistant   d. bullet

B Choose the correct form of the word to fill in the blanks.

1. He loved ____________ on the telephone.
   a. talkative   b. to talk   c. talker

2. She walked by ____________.
   a. casual   b. casualness   c. casually

3. It ____________ like it's been ages since I saw you.
   a. seems   b. seemingly   c. seeming

4. Peter started ____________.
   a. crybaby   b. crying   c. crier

5. He ____________ several experiments on electricity.
   a. conductor   b. conducted   c. conduction

Listening  T 46

Listen to the dialog and choose the best answer.

1. What is the lecture mainly about?
   a. The life of Alexander Graham Bell
   b. The invention of Graham Crackers
   c. The creation of the telephone
   d. The life of Thomas Watson

2. What did Bell do during the day?
   a. Sing to blind children
   b. Work in a company
   c. Attend school
   d. Teach deaf children

3. What did Watson do for Bell from 16 miles away?
   a. Sing and dance
   b. Read a news story and sing
   c. Tell a story
   d. Make a speech

Grammar Review

Choose the correct one.

1. ____________ foreign language is essentially a creative process.
   [Learn a / Learnt the / Learning a]

2. Many students were ____________ the musical.
   [interesting in / interested in / interesting at]

3. There was a serious accident, ____________ a tragedy.
   [which was / that was / that were]

4. ____________ this line of products, we considered many factors.
   [In to develop / In developed / In developing]

5. We couldn't ____________ at our own mistakes.
   [helped laugh / help laughing / helping laughing]

Vocabulary & Idioms

coast   *n.*   the land next to the sea, the seashore
      Ex.   *Several men were fishing on the coast.*

deck   *n.*   a platform extending horizontally from one side of a ship to the other
      Ex.   *The sailors were cleaning the deck.*

disastrous   *adj.*   causing great distress or injury, ruinous
      Ex.   *The disastrous wave crashed into the houses along the coast.*

consequence   *n.*   the effect, result, or outcome of a previous occurrence
      Ex.   *The thief suffered the consequences of going to jail and paying fines.*

outbreak   *n.*   a sudden and violent spontaneous occurrence
      Ex.   *The outbreak of the disease killed thousands.*

distrust   *v.*   to have no trust in
      Ex.   *After his horrible deed, he was distrusted by the people.*

possession   *n.*   anything owned or possessed
      Ex.   *The piano is my prize possession.*

interment camp   a camp for prisoners of war
      Ex.   *Finally, the prisoners were released from the internment camps.*

detention   *n.*   a state of being confined
      Ex.   *The students received detention for disrupting class.*

furnish   *v.*   to supply a building with necessary equipment
      Ex.   *I furnished my new apartment with tables and sofas.*

intern   *v.*   to restrict or confine
      Ex.   *The patient was interned at the hospital for a few days.*

compensate   *v.*   to give money to someone to make up for some loss
      Ex.   *The airlines compensated him for his discomfort on the airplane.*

A Choose the best word(s) to fill in the blank.

1. The captain called all the sailors to the main ___________.
   a. coast   b. outbreak   c. deck   d. consequence

2. The ___________ of cheering from the crowd surprised the speaker.
   a. consequences   b. internment   c. outbreak   d. coast

3. The ship reached the ___________ of Mexico.
   a. desert   b. mountains   c. coast   d. trees

4. Of course, the prisoners were taken to a ___________.
   a. palace   b. internment camp   c. restaurant   d. hotel

5. They were ___________ in a jailhouse.
   a. furnished   b. interned   c. lost   d. reasoned

B Choose the correct form of the word to fill in the blanks.

1. I ___________ her to strawberry-banana smoothies.
   a. introduction   b. introduced   c. introductory

2. I moved all my ___________ into my new house.
   a. possess   b. possessions   c. possessive

3. I didn't realize how hungry I ___________.
   a. been   b. was   c. being

4. The robbery was ___________ to the old man's business.
   a. disastrous   b. disaster   c. disastrousness

5. I was ___________ in a small room while the policeman asked me questions.
   a. interned   b. internship   c. intern

Listening  T47

Listen to the dialog and choose the best answer.

1. What is the lecture mainly about?
   a. The internment of Japanese Americans during the war
   b. The Wakatsuki's family business
   c. World War II
   d. Camp Manzanar

2. Why were Japanese Americans interned?
   a. They betrayed America.
   b. Their businesses were dangerous.
   c. Many Americans distrusted them.
   d. They had too many children.

3. Years after the war, the government decided to do what for the Japanese Americans?
   a. Continue to intern them
   b. Compensate them
   c. Banish them
   d. Deport them

Grammar Review

Choose the correct one.

1. Surprisingly, Mrs. Smith, ___________ strict teacher, attended the school festival.
   [which were/ that were/ who was a]

2. Having no time to lose, Sarah began ___________ her homework.
   [did/ to do/ do]

3. ___________ your parents love you, they cannot give you everything.
   [Even though/ Despite/ In spite of]

4. For security reasons, no one ___________ the basement.
   [were allowed enter/ were allowed entering/ was allowed to enter]

5. Finally, the government decided ___________ war against the communist country.
   [to declare/ declare/ declaring]

AFRICA'S MOST FAMOUS DESERT PEOPLE

Vocabulary & Idioms

desolate   *adj.*   barren or laid waste
Ex. *The desolate landscape had no grass or trees.*

toughest   *adj.*   most difficult
Ex. *This exam was the toughest I've ever taken.*

thrive   *v.*   to grow or develop vigorously, to prosper
Ex. *The climate is perfect for these animals to thrive.*

generation   *n.*   individuals born and living at the same time
Ex. *Our generation grew up listening to rock music.*

climate   *n.*   all weather conditions and patterns of a specific area
Ex. *The climate here is hot and dry.*

plunge   *v.*   to thrust forcibly into something that is penetrable
Ex. *The diver plunged into the water.*

hollow   *adj.*   having space or cavity inside
Ex. *The log is hollow.*

reed   *n.*   the straight stalk of a type of tall grass that grows in marshy areas
Ex. *We can use these reeds as straws to drink water.*

averse   *adj.*   having a strong feeling of opposition toward something
Ex. *Sam is averse to going out tonight.*

camouflage   *v.*   to disguise or hide by painting or screening objects
Ex. *The soldiers wore camouflaged clothing.*

creep   *v.*   to approach slowly and stealthily
Ex. *The tiger crept up behind the antelope preparing for attack.*

remote   *adj.*   far away, secluded
Ex. *The hermit lived in a remote cottage in the woods.*

Vocabulary Review

A **Choose the best word(s) to fill in the blank.**

1. The area is so ____________ that no animals are able to survive there.
   - a. remote
   - b. desolate
   - c. averse
   - d. favorable

2. The woodcutter cut out the inside of the log so that it was ____________.
   - a. hollow
   - b. remote
   - c. averse
   - d. desolate

3. I ____________ a straw into my cup.
   - a. thrived
   - b. camouflaged
   - c. plunged
   - d. crept

4. The ____________ of the mountains is much colder than that of the city.
   - a. generation
   - b. reed
   - c. climate
   - d. cloud

5. The burglar ____________ behind the shelf.
   - a. thrived
   - b. camouflaged
   - c. plunged
   - d. crept

B **Choose the correct form of the word to fill in the blanks.**

1. This is my very ____________ car.
   - a. ownership
   - b. owner
   - c. own

2. Let's go to the party ____________ him a happy birthday.
   - a. wishful
   - b. wisher
   - c. to wish

3. I don't mind ____________ with you.
   - a. gone
   - b. go-ahead
   - c. going

4. The man turned and ____________ at me.
   - a. look-alike
   - b. looked
   - c. looker

5. Always remember to look both ways before ____________ the street.
   - a. crossing
   - b. cross-cultural
   - c. cross-examine

Listen to the dialog and choose the best answer.

1. What is the lecture mainly about?
   a. Ostriches
   b. The San and their survival methods
   c. The Kalahari Desert
   d. The Sahara Desert

2. How do the San protect themselves from the powerful desert sun?
   a. They use sunscreen.
   b. They rub oil on themselves.
   c. They have a special diet.
   d. They pray to local gods.

3. How do the San obtain water in such a desert?
   a. They visit the ocean.
   b. They drink juice from nearby trees.
   c. They use reeds.
   d. They dig a well.

Grammar Review

Choose the correct one.

1. *War and Peace* is one of ____________ in history.
   [the greatest novel/ greater novels/ the greatest novels]

2. There are ____________ to make this world a better place for all.
   [much other way/ many other ways/ many other way]

3. ____________ Christie likes playing golf, her husband loves reading comics.
   [During/ While/ Because]

4. ____________ great efforts, you can achieve anything.
   [By making/ By make/ By to make]

5. ____________ all their attempts, they failed to climb the mountain.
   [Although/ Despite/ Because of]

Vocabulary & Idioms

tone	*n.*	a tint or shade, a quality of color
	Ex.	*Your shirt has a light green tone.*
classification	*n.*	the act of arranging or organizing by classes
	Ex.	*Scientists have many methods of classification.*
expert	*n.*	a person who has special skill or knowledge
	Ex.	*My father is a biology expert.*
precious	*adj.*	of high price or great value
	Ex.	*The necklace is very precious to Wendy.*
gemstone	*n.*	a precious or semiprecious stone
	Ex.	*The gemstone could be worth a lot of money.*
talc	*n.*	short for talcum, a soft mineral that has a soapy feel
	Ex.	*The product uses talc.*
mineral	*n.*	solid inorganic substances occurring in nature
	Ex.	*The ground is full of different minerals.*
calcite	*n.*	one of the materials that makes up limestone
	Ex.	*The stones are rich in calcite.*
file	*n.*	a long metal tool used to smooth surfaces of metal
	Ex.	*We used a file to smoothen the edges of the table.*
topaz	*n.*	a mineral that occurs in crystals and is used as a gemstone
	Ex.	*These gemstones are abundant with topaz.*
sapphire	*n.*	a clear type of gemstone that is usually blue
	Ex.	*Her husband gave her a beautiful sapphire ring.*
diamond	*n.*	a stone consisting of a pure, extremely hard carbon
	Ex.	*These diamonds are worth thousands of dollars.*

A Choose the best word(s) to fill in the blank.

1. How can I ever give up this ____________ photograph?

   a. gaudy   b. precious   c. cruel   d. averse

2. Describe the ____________ of the color to me.

   a. gemstone   b. tone   c. expert   d. file

3. To smooth the surface, we'll need a ____________.

   a. mineral   b. gemstone   c. file   d. diamond

4. He is an ____________ in mathematics.

   a. expert   b. artist   c. astronaut   d. optometrist

5. What is the ____________ system for plants?

   a. classification   b. talc   c. gemstone   d. tone

B Choose the correct form of the word to fill in the blanks.

1. We are ____________ his 15th birthday.

   a. celebrity   b. celebration   c. celebrating

2. The car ____________ to a sudden stop.

   a. brakeperson   b. brakeage   c. braked

3. He ____________ to sing until we reached our house.

   a. continuity   b. continued   c. continuous

4. Nobody paid ____________ to what we had to say.

   a. attention   b. attentive   c. attend

5. Scientists didn't know how to ____________ the species.

   a. classification   b. classify   c. classifiable

Listening  T49

Listen to the dialog and choose the best answer.

1. What is the lecture mainly about?
   a. Precious gemstones
   b. Geologists
   c. Rock experts
   d. The classification of rocks

2. How many classes exist in the classification system of rocks?
   a. 9   b. 20   c. 10   d. 8

3. What do scientists look at to determine which class a rock belongs to?
   a. The rock's tone
   b. The rock's hardness
   c. The rock's color
   d. The rock's shape

Grammar Review

Choose the correct one.

1. ______________ came to like the traditional methods of learning.

   [Most student/ Almost students/ Most students]

2. It is absolutely necessary to purchase ____________.

   [some new equipments/ some new equipment/ several new equipment]

3. Judy was ____________ she couldn't understand what their parents were saying.

   [so young that/ such young which/ so young what]

4. ____________ Dylan was the best player in his team, he couldn't compete in the race.

   [In spite/ During/ Although]

5. Many materials can ____________ make automobile parts.

   [being used/ be used to/ be using to]

Vocabulary & Idioms

military	*n.*	relating to the army or the armed forces
	Ex.	*My father joined the military when he was 20 years old.*
ambulance	*n.*	a vehicle used to carry injured people to a hospital
	Ex.	*We need to call an ambulance before your injury gets worse.*
civilian	*n.*	a person who is not on duty in the military
	Ex.	*Civilians lined the street cheering on the parade.*
principle	*n.*	a fundamental, primary, or general law of truth
	Ex.	*This class teaches the basic principles of physics.*
aloft	*adj.*	in or into the air
	Ex.	*The balloon floated aloft.*
curved	*adj.*	having or marked by a smoothly round bend
	Ex.	*The body of the car is curved.*
air pressure		a force exerted by air on the objects it comes in contact with
	Ex.	*What is the air pressure at sea level?*
rotor	*n.*	a rotating part of a machine
	Ex.	*The rotors continued to spin.*
lever	*n.*	a handle used to adjust or operate a mechanism
	Ex.	*These levers make the machine go up and down.*
hover	*v.*	to hang suspended in air
	Ex.	*The helicopter hovered overhead.*
tip over		to tilt, to cause or assume a slanting position
	Ex.	*Don't tip over the glass of water.*
certified	*adj.*	having or proved by a certificate, guaranteed
	Ex.	*I am a certified physician.*

Vocabulary Review

A Choose the best word(s) to fill in the blank.

1. The _____________ is preparing for an attack.
   a. military   b. ambulance   c. air pressure   d. civilian

2. Many _____________ were harmed by the explosion of the bomb.
   a. civilians   b. ambulances   c. levers   d. rotors

3. How does a hot air balloon stay _____________?
   a. curved   b. precious   c. huge   d. aloft

4. A few centuries ago scientists proved that the world was not flat but _____________.
   a. curved   b. precious   c. huge   d. aloft

5. The birds _____________ around the birdfeeder.
   a. burst   b. hovered   c. heeded   d. attacked

B Choose the correct form of the word to fill in the blanks.

1. There is too much _____________ at work.
   a. press   b. pressure   c. pressurize

2. The machine _____________ in a complicated way.
   a. functions   b. functional   c. functionally

3. That's _____________ what I'm trying to say.
   a. exact   b. exactness   c. exactly

4. _____________, we need to be healthy to function.
   a. Basic   b. Basically   c. Basics

5. Mastering taekwondo skills requires _____________.
   a. concentration   b. concentrate   c. concentrative

Listening  T50

Listen to the dialog and choose the best answer.

1. What is the lecture mainly about?
   a. How airplanes and helicopters fly
   b. How buses run
   c. Air pressure facts
   d. Fashion

2. What does a helicopter have that allows it to fly?
   a. Wings   b. Hot air
   c. Rotor blades   d. Fins

3. What is the phenomenon called that makes a helicopter fly?
   a. Drift   b. Thrust
   c. Punch   d. Lift

Grammar Review

Choose the correct one.

1. Michelle ____________ many tourist attractions since she came to Toronto.
   [visited/ visiting/ has visited]

2. Sometimes, people really wonder ____________.
   [who they are/ who are they/ they who are]

3. Fortunately, the prices remained ____________.
   [stably/ stable/ stableness]

4. If he ____________, tell him to wait for me.
   [will arrive/ arriving/ arrives]

5. A good teacher makes his or her students ____________ hard.
   [to study/ studied/ study]

Vocabulary & Idioms

illustrious	*adj.*	glorious, as deeds or work
	Ex.	*The famous inventor led an illustrious life.*
specifically	*adv.*	in distinction from others, particularly
	Ex.	*I specifically asked for mustard and not mayonnaise.*
directly	*adv.*	having no other factors involved, along a straight path
	Ex.	*He flew directly from Tokyo to Seoul.*
retreat	*v.*	to withdraw, especially for shelter or seclusion
	Ex.	*The army retreated to the base.*
festival	*n.*	a day of celebration
	Ex.	*We held a grand festival on Christmas Day.*
clown	*n.*	a comic performer, usually wearing ridiculous makeup
	Ex.	*We went to the circus to see the clowns.*
demon	*n.*	an evil spirit or devil
	Ex.	*It is rumored that the house is haunted by demons.*
personality	*n.*	the emotional characteristics of an individual
	Ex.	*He has a peculiar personality.*
role	*n.*	proper or customary function
	Ex.	*The policeman's role is to ensure safety.*
sprout	*v.*	to grow or develop
	Ex.	*The plants sprouted in the spring.*
carve	*v.*	to cut wood, stone, etc. into shape
	Ex.	*Sam carved a heart out of the piece of wood.*
culture	*n.*	the ideas, customs, and values of a particular society
	Ex.	*Cultures differ throughout the world.*

A Choose the best word(s) to fill in the blank.

1. The nation has an ____________ history.
   a. alien   b. illustrious   c. aqueous   d. omniscient

2. After school, I went ____________ home.
   a. specifically   b. accurately   c. directly   d. aromatically

3. An evil ____________ stirs around these parts.
   a. clown   b. demon   c. mother   d. chicken

4. The farmer is waiting for the beans to ____________.
   a. sprout   b. die   c. wither   d. jump

5. What ____________ does your father play in your household?
   a. personality   b. festival   c. demon   d. role

B Choose the correct form of the word to fill in the blanks.

1. He has a nice ____________.
   a. personal   b. personally   c. personality

2. The concept of order is ____________ to his philosophy.
   a. central   b. center   c. centrally

3. Her selfless service was ____________ by many people.
   a. recognition   b. recognized   c. recognizable

4. Doves are believed to ____________ peace.
   a. represent   b. representation   c. representative

5. My mother loves ____________ Christmas trees.
   a. decoration   b. decorating   c. decoratively

Listening  T51

Listen to the dialog and choose the best answer.

1. What is the lecture mainly about?
   a. Hopi Indians' diet
   b. Kachinas, a Native American custom
   c. Hopi festivals
   d. Hopi games

2. Where do kachinas retreat to during the winter?
   a. Lakes
   b. cities
   c. Faraway mountains
   d. California

3. What are kachinas?
   a. Animals
   b. Food
   c. Spirits
   d. Dragons

Grammar Review

Choose the correct one.

1. _____________ the winter, few people are willing to work outside.

   [Despite / Although / During]

2. In London, there are many places to visit, some _____________ are historically famous.

   [of which / at what / of them]

3. The sales were _____________ in the next quarter.

   [expected increasing / expected to increase / expecting to increase]

4. _____________ needs to practice as often as possible.

   [Each students / Every students / Each student]

5. As a society, we should help children _____________ potential.

   [realize their / realized them / realizing they]

Vocabulary & Idioms

naturalist   *n.*   someone who studies animal and plant life
Ex.   *Charles Darwin was a naturalist.*

enchanted   *adj.*   influenced by magic
Ex.   *The enchanted castle shined in the moonlight.*

isle   *n.*   a small island
Ex.   *The sailors saw an isle appear in the distance.*

species   *n.*   a group of organisms that are capable of interbreeding
Ex.   *The lion is one of the largest species of cats.*

evolve   *v.*   to develop from a primitive to a more advanced form
Ex.   *Animals have evolved over millions of years.*

adapt   *v.*   to change something to fit new circumstances
Ex.   *The plants adapted to the new temperatures.*

twig   *n.*   a small shoot or branch of a tree or bush
Ex.   *Let's pick up the leaves and twigs scattered around the yard.*

dive   *v.*   to throw oneself headfirst into the water
Ex.   *The swimmer dived into the pool.*

allow   *v.*   to permit someone to do something
Ex.   *The bird's wings allow it to fly and soar.*

tortoise   *n.*   a turtle that lives on land
Ex.   *Fred fed his pet tortoise lettuce.*

exceptionally   *adv.*   remarkably, outstandingly
Ex.   *The elephant has an exceptionally long nose.*

miniature   *adj.*   a small copy, model or breed of anything
Ex.   *Let's play miniature golf.*

Vocabulary Review

A Choose the best word(s) to fill in the blank.

1. These mountains are ______________ with beauty.
   a. miniature   b. listless   c. enchanted   d. adapting

2. The ______________ is surrounded on all sides by the Atlantic Ocean.
   a. twig   b. isle   c. naturalist   d. species

3. Although it looks like a turtle, the ______________ cannot swim.
   a. tortoise   b. dragon   c. lizard   d. tiger

4. The dolphin jumped and ______________ back into the ocean.
   a. evolved   b. allowed   c. dived   d. adapted

5. It's very hard for polar bears to ______________ to hot temperatures.
   a. evolve   b allow   c. dive   d. adapt

B Choose the correct form of the word to fill in the blanks.

1. The ______________ of humans took many years.
   a. evolution   b. evolve   c. evolutionary

2. My parents ______________ me to go to the movies with my friends.
   a. allowable   b. allowance   c. allowed

3. The researcher is a ______________.
   a. natural   b. naturalist   c. naturalism

4. He is ______________ good at writing.
   a. exception   b. exceptionally   c. except

5. Quality education is ______________ for producing good citizens.
   a. necessity   b. necessitates   c. necessary

Listen to the dialog and choose the best answer.

1. What is the lecture mainly about?
   a. The adaptation of a few Galapagos animals
   b. Galapagos food
   c. Types of Galapagos vegetation
   d. Galapagos natives

2. What did the tortoise grow in order to reach food?
   a. Large shells   b. Long necks
   c. Long legs   d. Sharp teeth

3. What does *galapagos* mean in Spanish?
   a. Lizard   b. Tortoise
   c. Finch   d. Lobster

Grammar Review

Choose the correct one.

1. Melanie didn't make it to the party ___________ missed the train.
   [because of her / because her / because she]

2. As a matter of fact, we need to learn ___________ a happy life.
   [why leads / how to lead / how leading]

3. There was once a frog ___________ did not like its mother.
   [what / whom / which]

4. Many farmers were ___________ their villages.
   [forced to leave / forcing to leave / forced leaving]

5. A large number of students were fascinated by ___________.
   [another stories / other story / another story]

Vocabulary & Idioms

wine   *n.*   an alcoholic drink made from fermenting fruit

             Ex.   *Phillip drinks a glass of wine daily.*

jazz   *n.*   a type of music with African American origins

             Ex.   *Jazz music was playing in the cafe.*

folk song   a song that has been passed down from generation to generation through oral tradition

             Ex.   *Do you know any Canadian folk songs?*

gospel   *n.*   lively religious music of African American origin

             Ex.   *I'm joining a gospel choir.*

incorporate   *v.*   to include

             Ex.   *The class incorporates many techniques.*

conventional   *adj.*   traditional, normal, customary

             Ex.   *Most conventional shops usually accept credit cards.*

sheet music   music written or printed on unbound sheets of paper

             Ex.   *Here's the sheet music for "Jingle Bells".*

spontaneously   *adv.*   instinctively

             Ex.   *He spontaneously made a speech to the entire class.*

improvise   *v.*   to perform music without preparing it in advance

             Ex.   *The performer improvised a song at the end of the show.*

clash   *v.*   to be unpleasing together

             Ex.   *These colors clash.*

great   *n.*   an important or distinguished person in a field

             Ex.   *He is one of the theatrical greats of France.*

theme   *n.*   a short melody that is the basis of a piece of music

             Ex.   *The theme of the song is lighthearted.*

A Choose the best word(s) to fill in the blank.

1. On Sundays, we sing ____________ in church.
   a. jazz   b. folk songs   c. hip hop   d. gospel

2. I'm having trouble reading the ____________ for this song.
   a. newspaper   b. novel   c. sheet music   d. gospel

3. The artist ____________ many flowers in his drawings.
   a. incorporates   b. clashes   c. recites   d. sings

4. The sound of trumpets playing ____________ with the birds' singing.
   a. incorporates   b. clashes   c. recites   d. sings

5. The song's ____________ is very sad.
   a. jazz   b. theme   c. sheet music   d. gospel

B Choose the correct form of the word to fill in the blanks.

1. ____________ European paintings are usually done with oil paint.
   a. Conventional   b. Convention   c. Conventionally

2. The music ____________ many traditional elements.
   a. combination   b. combinational   c. combines

3. The concept of ____________ intelligence is hard to define.
   a. emotional   b. emotion   c. emotionally

4. She ____________ responded to the awkward question.
   a. spontaneously   b. spontaneous   c. spontaneity

5. The article states that pollution is ____________.
   a. increasingly   b. increasing   c. increase

Listening  T53

Listen to the dialog and choose the best answer.

1. What is the lecture mainly about?
   a. Information about jazz music
   b. Louis Armstrong
   c. Jelly Roll Morton
   d. Southern black speech

2. Which two famous jazz artists were mentioned in the lecture?
   a. Bichet and Armstrong
   b. Armstrong and Morton
   c. Morton and Calloway
   d. Calloway and Bichet

3. Which of the following is NOT true according to the lecture?
   a. Jazz musicians made their instruments mimic human voices.
   b. Early jazz musicians wrote down their music.
   c. Jazz musicians typically start out playing melodies that listeners already know.
   d. Jazz never loses its roots.

Grammar Review

Choose the correct one.

1. His story ____________, but everybody just believed him.
   [seemed strangely/ seemed strange/ seeming strangely]

2. To our disappointment, we ____________ see Harold.
   [weren't able to/ was able to/ weren't ably]

3. His sad story made us ____________ a lot.
   [to cry/ cried/cry]

4. We can work together and ____________ a difference in the world.
   [made/ make/ making]

5. ____________ were walking along the street, we came across Susan.
   [During our/ While us/ As we]

Vocabulary & Idioms

routinely   *adv.*   ordinarily, normally
Ex.   I routinely exercise at night.

auction   *v.*   to sell something at a public sale to the person who offers the most money
Ex.   I auctioned off my used car for two thousand dollars.

appealing   *adj.*   attractive
Ex.   She wore a very appealing dress to the dinner party.

stare   *v.*   to look with a fixed gaze
Ex.   I stared at her in disbelief.

glare   *n.*   an angry stare
Ex.   He gave me a glare of anger.

self-portrait   *n.*   a portrait of oneself created by oneself
Ex.   The artist made a self-portrait.

accident   *n.*   an unexpected event that causes damage or harm
Ex.   Luckily, the accident was not serious.

rigid   *adj.*   stiff
Ex.   His body was rigid.

cast   *n.*   something made by molding
Ex.   The doctor put his broken arm in a cast.

recognition   *n.*   the acknowledgement of achievement, service, or merit
Ex.   He received recognition for his courage during the war.

gallery   *n.*   a room or series of room used to display art
Ex.   This is a gallery of all of Monet's most famous works.

museum   *n.*   a building where arts, scientific specimens, or other objects of permanent value are kept
Ex.   We went to the museum to see the dinosaur bones.

Vocabulary Review

A Choose the best word(s) to fill in the blank.

1. The farmer ______________ off his tractor.
   a. stared   b. auctioned   c. joked   d. lifted

2. I ______________ at the sunset for a few minutes.
   a. stared   b. auctioned   c. joked   d. lifted

3. The car ______________ injured many people.
   a. accident   b. self-portrait   c. recognition   d. cast

4. I am painting a[n] ______________.
   a. accident   b. self-portrait   c. recognition   d. cast

5. The soldier stood ______________ at attention.
   a. visually   b. carelessly   c. merrily   d. rigidly

B Choose the correct form of the word to fill in the blanks.

1. Teddy ______________ eats chicken for lunch at work.
   a. routine   b. routinely   c. route

2. Your hat is very ______________.
   a. appealing   b. appealer   c. appeal

3. Who was the last person ______________ the room?
   a. entrance   b. entry   c. to enter

4. The concept of logic is ______________ in many respects.
   a. complication   b. complicated   c. complicate

5. Her neck was ______________ injured.
   a. severity   b. severe   c. severely

  T54

Listen to the dialog and choose the best answer.

1. What is the lecture mainly about?
   a. One work of art by Kahlo
   b. European artwork
   c. Mexican women
   d. Latin American politics

2. How did Frida's painting compare to the European paintings that were sold for a similar price?
   a. It was heavier.
   b. It was more complex.
   c. It was brighter.
   d. It was smaller.

3. What gave Frida's painting much of its appeal?
   a. The Mexican woman's intense glare
   b. The dull colors
   c. The landscape
   d. The price

Grammar Review

Choose the correct one.

1. ______________ made it a success was its focus on customer satisfaction.
   [That/ Whose/ What]

2. Lots of people ______________ injured in the collision.
   [were badly/ was bad/ were badness]

3. The artist ______________ friends with many famous people since 2005.
   [making/ has made/ made]

4. There are many dangerous things ______________ can affect our lives.
   [who/ what/ which]

5. ______________ up in South Korea, Sally became interested in taekwondo.
   [While growing/ During grown/ While grows]

Vocabulary & Idioms

moth
n. an insect similar to a butterfly but usually seen at night
Ex. *Several moths hovered around the streetlight.*

dizzy
adj. having a sensation of spinning and a tendency to fall
Ex. *The car ride made him a little bit dizzy.*

logical
adj. reasonable
Ex. *There is a logical answer to our problem.*

ray
n. a narrow beam of light
Ex. *The sun's rays felt warm.*

parallel
adj. going in the same direction and never converging
Ex. *These two roads are parallel.*

angle
n. the figure formed by two lines diverging from a common point
Ex. *The plane flew in at an angle.*

ensure
v. to guarantee, to make sure
Ex. *The guards ensured the king's safety.*

philosophy
n. a system of guidance in practical affairs
Ex. *My philosophy is to always eat as much as possible during a meal.*

automatically
adv. in a reflex manner
Ex. *The door shuts automatically.*

course
n. a direction or route taken
Ex. *We followed the course of the stream.*

disoriented
adj. confused as to time or place
Ex. *The accident left him disoriented.*

distract
v. to draw away or divert, as the mind or attention
Ex. *She was too distracted to study.*

A Choose the best word(s) to fill in the blank.

1. The ______________ flew circles around the lamp.
   a. motif   b. fabric   c. rays   d. moth

2. I could see ______________ of light on the highway.
   a. motif   b. fabric   c. rays   d. moth

3. The two lines are ______________.
   a. logical   b. automatic   c. disoriented   d. parallel

4. Nothing can ______________ that our business will definitely be a success.
   a. distract   b. ensure   c. divert   d. entice

5. The ship's ______________ was set for Europe.
   a. course   b. rays   c. moth   d. fabric

B Choose the correct form of the word to fill in the blanks.

1. Is this an ______________ door?
   a. automatic   b. automatically   c. automate

2. The noise was very ______________.
   a. distraction   b. distracting   c. distract

3. I felt ______________ after running the marathon.
   a. disorientation   b. disorient   c. disoriented

4. Please explain your ______________ to me.
   a. philosophy   b. philosophical   c. philosophically

5. There must be a ______________ explanation.
   a. logic   b. logical   c. logically

Listening  T55

Listen to the dialog and choose the best answer.

1. What is the lecture mainly about?
   a. The moon's light
   b. A moth's flight pattern
   c. Artificial lights
   c. A moth's body structure

2. What distracts a moth?
   a. The moon
   b. The sun
   c. Its reflection
   d. An artificial light

3. While distracted, the moth flies in ____________.
   a. circles
   b. squares
   c. parallel lines
   d. triangles

Grammar Review

Choose the correct one.

1. That was the reason ____________ Eric quit the job.
   [when / why / what]

2. We're just trying ____________ our lives.
   [to improve / to improving / improved]

3. We are going to throw a party ____________ everybody can have fun.
   [such what / so that / so when]

4. The fact is ____________ no students want to visit the museum.
   [what / whether / that]

5. Everybody became ____________ the enticing story.
   [interesting in / interested in / interesting at]

Vocabulary & Idioms

unravel   *v.*   to undo, make plain or clear
Ex.   *The mystery was unraveled.*

document   *n.*   any written item of a factual or informative nature
Ex.   *You need to present a legal document such as a passport.*

shepherd   *n.*   a person who herds, tends, and guards sheep
Ex.   *An old shepherd worked in the field.*

scroll   *n.*   a roll of parchment, paper, etc. that has writing on it
Ex.   *The priest unrolled and read the scrolls.*

postage   *n.*   the charge for mailing an item
Ex.   *How much is the postage for sending a package to Wisconsin?*

scholar   *n.*   a learned person who has profound knowledge on a subject
Ex.   *He is a scholar of Greek history.*

collect   *v.*   to gather together, to assemble
Ex.   *I collect bottles as a hobby.*

translate   *v.*   to turn from one language into another
Ex.   *My French teacher translated the paragraph from French to English.*

author   *n.*   a person who writes a novel, poem, essay, etc.
Ex.   *Who is the author of this novel?*

holy   *adj.*   declared sacred by religious use or authority
Ex.   *Let's all open our Holy Bibles.*

partially   *adv.*   not completely
Ex.   *The pizza was partially eaten.*

treasure   *n.*   anything a person greatly values or highly prizes
Ex.   *This monument is a national treasure.*

Vocabulary Review

A Choose the best word(s) to fill in the blank.

1. I am trying to ______________ my shoelaces.
   a. collect   b. unravel   c. rip   d. chew

2. Can you please ______________ this into Spanish for me?
   a. collect   b. unravel   c. rip   d. translate

3. The ______________ examined the artifacts for his research.
   a. scholar   b. shepherd   c. author   d. policeman

4. Please help me ______________ all the rocks in the yard.
   a. collect   b. unravel   c. rip   d. chew

5. J.K. Rowling is a famous ______________.
   a. shepherd   b. author   c. policeman   d. waiter

B Choose the correct form of the word to fill in the blanks.

1. I ______________ finished my homework.
   a. part   b. partial   c. partially

2. Did you pay for ______________?
   a. postal   b. posting   c. postage

3. Do you have all the ______________ ready?
   a. documents   b. documentable   c. documentary

4. The children were ______________ by the film.
   a. fascination   b. fascinated   c. fascinate

5. The ______________ details of the accident were not revealed.
   a. exact   b. exactly   c. exactitude

Listen to the dialog and choose the best answer.

1. What is the lecture mainly about?
   a. The Dead Sea Scrolls   b. Postage stamps
   c. Various religions   d. The Dead Sea

2. What are the three languages in which the Dead Sea Scrolls were written?
   a. English, Chinese, and French
   b. Greek, Aramaic, and French
   c. Greek, Aramaic, and Hebrew
   d. Hebrew, Chinese, and English

3. What were the Dead Sea Scrolls?
   a. Religious writings   b. An addendum to the Bible
   c. Muslim prayers   d. Native American poems

Grammar Review

Choose the correct one.

1. There _____________ a serious accident in 1997.
   [has been/ are/ was]

2. Tom was fond of a girl _____________ lived in a big house.
   [who/ whose/ whom]

3. _____________ nobody wanted to come to the party, it was called off.
   [Since/ Although/ Whether]

4. We live in a town _____________ we can feel safe.
   [when/ why/ where]

5. No one knew _____________.
   [how was the woman/ who the woman was/ why was the woman]

Vocabulary & Idioms

attention	*n.*	notice or awareness
	Ex.	*The disturbance caught the policeman's attention.*
map	*v.*	to represent or delineate on or as if on a map
	Ex.	*Early sailors mapped the Mississippi River.*
echo	*n.*	a repetition of sound caused by the reflection of sound
	Ex.	*My voice echoed in the mountains.*
depth	*n.*	the extent, measurement or dimension downward
	Ex.	*The depth of the ocean here is around three miles deep.*
canyon	*n.*	a deep gorge with steep sides
	Ex.	*Have you ever been to the Grand Canyon?*
chain	*n.*	a series of closely connected things
	Ex.	*The mountain chain ran for miles.*
ton	*n.*	an American unit of weight equal to 2,000 lbs.
	Ex.	*This must weigh a ton.*
submarine	*n.*	a vessel designed for underwater travel
	Ex.	*German submarines patrolled the waters.*
vessel	*n.*	a craft for traveling in or on water
	Ex.	*The navy prepared its vessels for war.*
withstand	*v.*	to resist
	Ex.	*The knight's armor withstood the thrusts of his opponent's spear.*
searchlight	*n.*	a lamp and reflector that throws a powerful beam
	Ex.	*It was so dark we needed a searchlight.*
porthole	*n.*	a window in a ship or an airplane
	Ex.	*I looked out the porthole.*

A Choose the best word(s) to fill in the blank.

1. Did you pay _____________ to the sign?
   a. convention   b. detention   c. attention   d. tribute

2. Have you ever measured the _____________ of this pool?
   a. depression   b. depot   c. deposit   d. depth

3. The load weighs about two _____________.
   a. vessels   b. tons   c. atoms   d. echoes

4. I can't _____________ his insults.
   a. map   b. withstand   c. amuse   d. list

5. The _____________ of ants marched steadily, one after another.
   a. vessel   b. depth   c. chain   d. mark

B Choose the correct form of the word to fill in the blanks.

1. It is _____________ that Marianne succeeded.
   a. remarkably   b. remarkable   c. remark

2. All of us are _____________ of the danger of pollution.
   a. aware   b. awareness   c. award

3. In fact, it is difficult to _____________ the distance.
   a. measurement   b. measure   c. measurable

4. We _____________ something bizarre.
   a. noticeable   b. noticeably   c. noticed

5. Of course, nuclear arsenals are _____________ powerful.
   a. extreme   b. extremity   c. extremely

Listening   🔊 T57

Listen to the dialog and choose the best answer.

1. What is the lecture mainly about?
   a. Echo sounders
   b. Ocean life
   c. The Mariana Trench
   d. The Mariana Islands

2. How long did it take for the scientists to reach the bottom of the trench?
   a. Five hours
   b. Nineteen hours
   c. Ten hours
   d. Nine hours

3. What did the scientists use to discover the trench?
   a. Echo sounders
   b. Wave detectors
   c. Submarine radar
   d. Searchlights

Grammar Review

Choose the correct one.

1. Toronto is famous _____________ the largest city in Canada.
   [as be/ by been/ for being]

2. We went to a restaurant _____________ in Elm Street.
   [locating/ located/ locate]

3. In fact, the area is _____________.
   [extremely dangerous/ extreme dangerous/ extreme dangerously]

4. Ten days later, Maggie managed to _____________ Boston.
   [reach to/ reach/ reached]

5. _____________ they found out was quite interesting.
   [That/ If/ What]

Krakatoa

Vocabulary & Idioms

dormant	*adj.*	inactive
	Ex.	*The volcano was dormant.*
rock	*v.*	to sway or make something sway back and forth
	Ex.	*The mother rocked her baby to sleep.*
sink	*v.*	to fall or cause to fall
	Ex.	*The boat was beginning to sink.*
aftermath	*n.*	the results of something, usually a great and terrible event
	Ex.	*The aftermath of the war was terrible.*
ash	*n.*	dusty residue that remains after something is burnt
	Ex.	*The fire left ashes everywhere.*
air current		airflow
	Ex.	*The birds floated with the air current.*
degree	*n.*	a measurement of temperature in Celsius or Fahrenheit
	Ex.	*The temperature is a few degrees hotter today than yesterday.*
overturn	*v.*	to turn something or be turned upside down
	Ex.	*The wave overturned the ships.*
tidal	*adj.*	describing the rise and fall of waves
	Ex.	*The surfers surfed along the tidal waves.*
wipe out		to completely destroy, eliminate
	Ex.	*We wiped out the termites in our house.*
tsunami	*n.*	a large and fast-moving wave
	Ex.	*The weatherman says there may be a tsunami approaching.*
comeback	*n.*	a return to former success
	Ex.	*Will the retired star be able to make a comeback?*

Vocabulary Review

A Choose the best word(s) to fill in the blank.

1. How hot is the weather in ____________ Celsius?
   a. degrees   b. air currents   c. inches   d. meters

2. The tornado's ____________ was worse.
   a. bulk   b. aftermath   c. tsunami   d. ash

3. Let's clean up the ____________ in the fireplace.
   a. ashes   b. comeback   c. pints   d. degrees

4. A large ____________ crashed into boats and overturned them.
   a. tsunami   b. lever   c. degree   d. porthole

5. The ship ____________ into the ocean.
   a. rocked   b. sank   c. wiped out   d. returned

B Choose the correct form of the word to fill in the blanks.

1. The ____________ waves were small.
   a. tide   b. tiding   c. tidal

2. Actually, the ____________ was predictable.
   a. explode   b. explosion   c. explosively

3. That was a ____________ matter to discuss.
   a. serious   b. seriously   c. seriousness

4. I hope the medicine will ____________ the pain.
   a. less   b. lesser   c. lessen

5. Unfortunately, ____________ 200 people were killed in the accident.
   a. approximate   b. approximation   c. approximately

Listen to the dialog and choose the best answer.

1. What is the lecture mainly about?
   a. The falling of world temperatures
   b. Mount Krakatoa's eruption and its aftermath
   c. Krakatoa village people
   d. The Earth's complex atmosphere

2. What happened to the volcano after the eruptions stopped?
   a. It became dormant again.   b. It sank into the ocean.
   c. It grew larger.   d. It was covered in snow.

3. What happened to world temperatures following the eruption?
   a. They grew dryer.   b. They grew warmer
   c. They grew more humid.   d. They grew cooler.

Grammar Review

Choose the correct one.

1. A gentleman ______________ Paul Smith came to see you.
   [called/ calling/ calls]

2. Before he came to Tokyo, Kevin ______________ in San Diego.
   [lives/ had lived/ has lived]

3. Unfortunately, things ______________.
   [got badly/ gotten worse/ got worse]

4. Erica ______________ a good girl.
   [used to being/ used to be/ was used to be]

5. We were proud of ______________ sacrified themselves.
   [those what/ that which/ those who]

Vocabulary & Idioms

essential   *adj.*   absolutely necessary

    Ex. A nutritious diet is essential to good health.

vastly   *adv.* greatly, considerably

    Ex. He is vastly better at it than he was before.

sign language   a form of communication that uses gestures to represent words and ideas

    Ex. They communicated in sign language.

refer   *v.*   to regard as belonging to a particular class

    Ex. This type of color is referred to as turquoise.

clumsy   *adj.* badly or awkwardly made

    Ex. Her work was clumsy.

construct   *v.*   to build, form or put together

    Ex. The manager constructed a new schedule for the employees.

distinct   *adj.* clear, easily perceived by the senses

    Ex. I heard a distinct sound.

proper   *adj.* correct, appropriate

    Ex. What is the proper way to pronounce this word?

element   *n.*   part, component

    Ex. Coordination is an important element of athleticism.

expression   *n.*   the look on the face that shows feelings

    Ex. His expression was happy.

mere   *adj.* no more than

    Ex. It's a mere two centimeters long.

ignore   *v.*   to deliberately take no notice of

    Ex. I ignored his insults.

A Choose the best word(s) to fill in the blank.

1. He made a disgusted ____________ when he noticed the smell of trash.
   a. element   b. sign language   c. portrait   d. expression

2. Sara's voice was loud and ____________.
   a. mere   b. clumsy   c. tidal   d. distinct

3. She wore a[n] ____________ looking dress that made her look awkward.
   a. mere   b. clumsy   c. tidal   d. essential

4. He speaks ____________ English.
   a. mere   b. essential   c. proper   d. tidal

5. I communicated with the deaf old man through ____________.
   a. sign language   b. construction
   c. elements   d. announcements

B Choose the correct form of the word to fill in the blanks.

1. I looked out at the ____________ fields of Kentucky.
   a. vast   b. vastly   c. vastness

2. We were told to ____________ a flower out of paper.
   a. construction   b. constructive   c. construct

3. He ____________ to me as Cool Pete.
   a. reference   b. refers   c. referral

4. There are ____________ kinds of flowers on that island.
   a. variety   b. variously   c. various

5. I need your ____________.
   a. attention   b. attend   c. attentive

Listening  T59

Listen to the dialog and choose the best answer.

1. What is the lecture mainly about?
   a. Different kinds of sign language
   b. Hand and body symbols
   c. Facial expressions
   d. American Sign Language

2. Which of the following is NOT an element of ASL?
   a. Hand symbols
   b. Body language
   c. Finger muscles
   d. Facial expressions

3. ASL is short for ______________.
   a. American Sign Language
   b. African Sign Language
   c. American Sign Logic
   d. Australian System Logic

Grammar Review

Choose the correct one.

1. ______________ the storm, we couldn't gain access to the village.
   [Because/ Even though/ Because of]

2. Water is ______________ hydrogen and oxygen.
   [make up/ made up of/ making up by]

3. ______________, Alice felt extremely happy.
   [While singing/ Despite her sung/ While sing]

4. In reality, the world ______________.
   [has constantly changing/ is constantly changing/ has constantly change]

5. First of all, you need to understand how ______________.
   [was it constructed/ would it construct/ it was constructed]

Vocabulary & Idioms

primitive   *adj.*   relating to the earliest times
Ex.   *The cavemen built primitive dwellings.*

ancestor   *n.*   someone more distant than a grandparent
Ex.   *My ancestors are from Ireland.*

resemble   *v.*   to be like or similar to
Ex.   *Freddy resembles his sister.*

bulging   *adj.*   swollen, curving outward
Ex.   *He flexed his bulging muscles.*

ridge   *n.*   a long, narrow, or crested part of the body
Ex.   *Her glasses slid down the ridge of her nose.*

bare   *adj.*   lacking furnishings or equipment
Ex.   *The walls of the house were bare.*

merge   *v.*   to blend or combine with something else
Ex.   *The roads merge up ahead.*

dialect   *n.*   a form of language spoken in a particular region
Ex.   *The people in this area speak a different dialect.*

furthermore   *adv.*   in addition to what is being said
Ex.   *Furthermore, he is able to speak three other languages.*

bury   *v.*   to place in a grave
Ex.   *We buried the dead goldfish.*

vanish   *v.*   to disappear or cease to exist
Ex.   *The pain vanished.*

inventive   *adj.*   creative, resourceful
Ex.   *Thomas Edison had an inventive nature.*

Vocabulary Review

A Choose the best word(s) to fill in the blank.

1. My _____________ moved to America hundreds of years ago.
   a. descendants b. ancestors c. offspring d. heirs

2. The two groups _____________ and became one large group.
   a. resembled b. merged c. buried d. vanished

3. They are speaking in a southern _____________.
   a. ridge b. ancestor c. dialect d. element

4. This is the cemetery where my great grandfather is _____________.
   a. resembled b. merged c. buried d. vanished

5. He caught the ball with his _____________ hands.
   a. mere b. bare c. proper d. distinct

B Choose the correct form of the word to fill in the blanks.

1. It takes an _____________ mind.
   a. invention b. inventive c. inventor

2. What we need badly is more _____________ information.
   a. specifically b. specification c. specific

3. The ghost _____________ into thin air.
   a. vanishment b. vanished c. vanishingly

4. The two brothers _____________ each other.
   a. resemble b. resemblance c. resembling

5. Her stomach was _____________.
   a. bulge b. bulged c. bulging

Listen to the dialog and choose the best answer.

1. What is the lecture mainly about?
   a. Neanderthals
   b. Humans
   c. Hunting
   d. Funeral rituals

2. According to the lecture, the Neanderthals could make tools from what material?
   a. Wood
   b. Stone
   c. Plastic
   d. Metal

3. Which of the following is NOT true about Neanderthals?
   a. They completely died out.
   b. They were unintelligent.
   c. They hunted in small groups.
   d. They buried the dead.

Grammar Review

Choose the correct one.

1. Millions of years ago, most people ______________ caves.
   [have lived at/ live/ lived in]

2. Jessica ______________ her grandfather.
   [resembles/ resembles after/ resembled after]

3. The new strategy was ______________ than the old one.
   [more effectively/ much more effective/ much effective]

4. ______________ made a terrible mistake, he was willing to fix it.
   [Despite his/ When him/ Although he]

5. ______________ writing the book, Anna comforted herself.
   [Finish/ Having finished/ Finished]

Build**Up**
Reading Level 2

Workbook